Bursting The Bubble - The Story of Being 'Lost Without Her'

Bursting The Bubble - The Story of Being 'Lost Without Her'

A book about growing through tragedy & loss

MARK OBORN

Published by Mark Oborn

First Printing, 2020

ISBN print 978-1-5272-6418-2
ISBN digital 978-1-5272-6419-9

www.lost-without-her.com/

Contents

For Claire

You worked as a counsellor for the National Childbirth Trust, you loved helping others.

You did a psychology degree with the Open University to find out more about how our mind worked, you loved helping others.
You began a Masters Degree in Therapeutic Counselling yet died before you completed it, you loved helping others.
And now this book is written in your memory, with your help, with your love and through this book you continue to help others, for ever.

For Claire

Introduction

I am an organised person.

I run my own business helping dentists with their marketing and I have trained as a business and life coach so I have (correction, 'had') a great big life goal.

We were going to grow old together, we were going to live in a house by the sea, working only two days a week each and spending the remainder of the time travelling the UK & Europe in our campervan with our little dog.

The house was on the market, we had found a new one 15 minutes walk from the beach, we'd been to look at some campervans and last year we bought our little dog – it was all slowly coming together after the years we had dedicated to bringing up our 4 beautiful children.

And then she died.

My bubble burst.

My name is Mark and I had been married to the wonderful Claire for 22 years, we had even been dating six years before that since we were 16 years old. We only ever had each other and we were the love of each other's lives.

Claire was 43 and had been in good health, so we thought, but on 17 April 2013 she woke up with a headache and mild sickness, we'd been for a curry the night before to celebrate my birthday and so weren't overly concerned. By 10:30 she was vomiting heavily and took to her bed. When I got home from work at 17:30 she was so ill that her sister, who was visiting, decided to take her to the local hospital accident and emergency.

By 18:30 she had had a cardiac arrest and was on a ventilator, they sedated her and took her for a CT scan for her head and stomach to find out what the problem was.

She never made it to the scan as she had another cardiac arrest, and by 19:30 she was gone. The doctors fought to save her but because she deteriorated so rapidly they had absolutely no idea what was wrong with her and so had no way of treating her. Turns out she had a tumor, a phaeochromocytoma, the 'time bomb tumour'!

So where does that leave me now? It leaves me with the largest hole in my life that I have ever known and leads me on a journey to rebuilding my 'assumed future', to understanding why my bubble burst, what the bubble is and how it can be rebuilt... In fact, should it be rebuilt?

We all build bubbles around our lives, we build bubbles of assumptions about what will happen, we build bubbles that tell us everything will be okay, we build bubbles that give the world meaning, we build bubbles around the security of our marriage, we build bubbles around the security of other relationships... And sometimes those bubbles burst.

When my bubble burst I took to writing as my therapy and this book is the journal I kept on that journey.

This book is for you if you have lost a 'significant other'. This book is for you if you find yourself on a journey through grief, or are supporting someone else through their journey.

The book charts my first year of being a widower, its chapters are a series of blog posts I wrote immediately after Claire died, you can read all of those posts here http://lost-without-her.com. If you like any particular post please feel free to visit the original website and comment. To do this, visit the website, locate the search box and search for the blog post title.

This book is ordered chronologically by days, then weeks then months, this allows you to dip into any time after your event which feels relevant to you and see what I was saying and thinking *at that same time*. It's important to stress that '....*at that same time*' is really important. After 7 years it may not be how I feel now, in fact, I might even give my past self a good talking to if I could for some of the things written here. However, I feel it's more important to reproduce this 'as I felt at that time', it truly is a lesson in how far I have come and how far you might go as you walk your journey with me.

Each blog post I wrote and therefore each chapter in this book is tagged, the website is searchable by each of those tags and I've used the same tags here for each chapter. The tags represent feelings, emotions and events. If you go to the index at the back of the book you can find those tags or themes and discover which of the chapters/blog posts will be most relevant to how you are feeling right now.

As with the blog, I feel like I'm with you on your journey as you read this book... Just know you are not alone.

1. Day 0

The love of my life, my friend, my soulmate dies...

2. Days 1 & 2 Immediate Loss

Days 1 & 2

Too painful.
  Numb.
  No thoughts.
  No feelings.
  Nothing.

3. Day 3 The Sun is shining

The sun was shining this morning and that was the first time since Claire died, it wasn't a sign or anything like that, but I just noticed the change in weather. The grief comes in huge waves, and all it needs is a simple trigger like the sun coming out... there seems to be no reason for it, no explanation and no way to stop it.

The kids are the same. Olivia (eldest daughter – 18) went to Tesco for some supplies and came back upset as it was always Claire that took her to the shops. We all have our own triggers that set us off!

Yesterday Olivia was struggling with a picture she had in her mind of Claire in the Chapel of Rest. I didn't go but Claire's Mum and Dad & Sister went and Olivia thought it might help her too. All she could see in her mind was Claire in the Chapel of Rest – I think she thought she'd look like she was simply asleep and was disturbed to find that Claire looked very different. I have a good friend that is a Master NLP & Hypnosis Coach, so she popped over to 'mess with that picture' in Olivia's head and replace it with a nice happy one. It worked a treat!

My challenge today

Today it's been the realisation that I'll never have one of 'our' conversations again. We were both very much in to psychology – Claire from a formal educative background (She had a Bsc Hons in Psychology and was part way through an Msc in Counselling

Psycholology) and me from a Neuro Linguistic Programming and Hypnosis angle.

We'd talk deeply about how some people 'project' on to others, and how important it is to become 'self aware' at an early point in life. We both knew that most people never understand either of those concepts... we both did and could talk for hours.

We just 'got' each other. There was such a deep understanding between us that has developed over the past 30 years together and I miss those conversations where we could both offload so much.. I so want to offload what's on my mind right now and the only person in the world I can do that with isn't here. The pain is just so immense right now.

My progress today

I slept last night and got some respite from the pain.

Tagged

· Triggers

4. Day 4 Work has to change

0830 – I run 2 of my own companies, a marketing company and coaching company. Things need to change now. I was always able to work overseas or far away if needed, Claire was always supportive and didn't mind me being away – she was one of life's 'copers' who coped with ANYTHING – nothing was ever too much bother for her and she knew that my success would help us achieve our dreams (perhaps I'll write about those sometime, but as yet that is too painful to consider).

If I am away who is going to sort out the kids? They need picking up and dropping off. Work has to change.

1030 – I've just taken the dog for a walk, a bright sunny day but I feel so, so, so empty. Almost like the worst hunger pain I've ever felt but just no way to get any sustenance. I love her so much.

1300 – I started writing this blog. A welcome distraction

I've also started to notice people posting to Claire's Facebook page, telling her they love her and what a great friend she was. The kids are also posting each day talking to their mum.

Each time I read those posts I cry, they make me realise what a GREAT Mum she was and such a positive influence on other people too.

A tough day today...

5. Day 5 Decisions, decisions

Morning

Claire made all the decisions in our house, and like any good husband I just went along with them. It made for an easy life for both of us, there was never any friction... I just did what Claire told me to do and if she was happy I was happy.

But where do I go now to make decisions?

I feel completely lost today, like a directionless, headless chicken – wildly spinning in every direction.

Claire would have known what to do.

On the subject of decisions that Claire made. She booked a holiday for us all in July... but I've no idea where, how to pay the balance, who to contact or who in the family she booked it for!

Afternoon

I've done some work today. On the one hand it seems wrong that I just get on with things as if nothing has happened, but on the other hand it is a blessed relief and I can feel my mind welcoming the opportunity to light up some different neural pathways and think about something else.

Getting back to some work has really helped this afternoon. I think getting 'a' routine back is going to be really important – it just feels so wrong doing it without Claire!

Biggest Challenge today

Sorting out answer phone messages. Our good friend Katie popped over and sorted the answer phone messages out, there was one from Claire on there from last week which stung... thank you Katie for sorting that out for me...

tagged

- Decisions

6. Day 6 Peace

Last night I was talking to a good friend of mine Kevin Rose (thanks for the call mate, it really helped), we were just talking it all through – how we're coping and what happened to Claire. During that conversation I really felt an immense feeling of peace.

Peace that we told each other we loved each other often.

Peace that we never left anything unsaid.

Peace that we never argued and rarely even disagreed.

Peace that we have no regrets in our relationship.

Peace that Claire lived this way with all her friends and family, she died at total rest and harmony with the world.

My sweetheart you continue to inspire me each day.

tagged

- Peace

7. Day 7 Devotion

People are saying that it's lovely that Claire and I were devoted to one another. We were, absolutely and totally. But that was starting to leave a hole for me thinking that way, devotion to me means having someone there to receive it... and she's not!

I was devoted to listening to her and now I can't

I was devoted to being there for her and now I can't be

I was devoted to providing for her and now I can't

I have a choice, I can choose to keep thinking that way and life won't get better, or I can choose to redefine what devotion means to me.

Someone sent me this yesterday (Thank you Castle Way Dental Practice), it made me cry but this is what devotion now means to me and I'm going to live life this way:

> You can shed tears that she is gone or you can smile because she has lived.
>
> You can close your eyes and pray that she'll come back or you can open your eyes and see all she's left.
>
> Your heart can be empty because you can't see her or you can be full of the love you shared.
>
> You can turn your back on tomorrow and live yesterday or you can be happy for tomorrow because of yesterday.
>
> You can remember her and only that she's gone or you can cherish her memory and let it live on.
>
> You can cry and close your mind, be empty and turn your back or you can do what she'd want: smile, open your eyes, love and go on.

OK, I gotta go back to work because that's set me off again...

tagged

· Devotion

8. Day 8 Feeling cold

I feel so lonely today. Almost like my emotional central heating system has been shut down – there's a 'chill inside' which seems to need the flame that was Claire to warm it up. So what can I do?

You know, writing this blog is SO helpful – it makes sense of those weird feelings, I just start writing and see where it goes.

So back to my 'chill inside' analogy.

As an a-typical woman Claire often turned the heating down to save a few pennies – when I mentioned it was cold she used to say 'put on another jumper then' – so all I need to do is to find some extra emotional clothing and I'll be warm again – aahhh shit... I'm off crying again!

OK, it's now a few hours later and I've got myself together again: I've no idea where or what that emotional clothing is or looks like but what I do know for sure is this:

I am in control of what I choose to think and how I think it, therefore I can change what and how I think

I have all the resources I need to 'warm up' – I may not know how to access them right now, but I know they are there, and with the support of my family and friends (and indeed writing this) I know I will find them.

Just writing that down helps.

At the moment I'm cold, but it's actually comforting to know that I can and will be warm again – and that I have everything I need to do it.

Tagged

- Feeling cold

9. Day 9 Blurred, Confused & Timeless

I've not put the day on this post as I'm getting lost – I write these in the morning, so I'm getting confused about which day I'm talking about – was it yesterday that was day 9 or today?

My thinking is blurred and the days are blending in to one confused and timeless blob.

I've been through Claire's diary to get the house and kids sorted with what to do each day... and being a techy geek I've set it up as separate Google Calendar, synced it to my phone and the kids' phones so we all share it – and integrated it in to my work's diary so I know when I can commit to certain events etc... Trust the system Mark, trust the system.

Today I'm arranging the funeral, Dad's coming with me as support. Thanks Mum and Dad, you've been so good this past week.

Hopefully by the end of today I'll be able to give you a date.

I sat down with the 4 kids last night and discussed the funeral and what they wanted to do, a few tears were shed but we came up with an idea that will put a smile on their faces and on those that attend – I want all memories for the kids to be good ones, and that includes the funeral.

tagged

- Blurred
- Confused
- Funeral

- I'm a geek

10. Day 10 Funeral arrangement

I arranged the funeral yesterday – thanks Dad for coming with me. It is on Friday 3rd May at 1000 at the Chiltern Crematorium in Amersham – everyone is welcome.

It was surreal, almost like it was happening to someone else. In fact the the whole day yesterday was surreal – I registered Claire's death and that didn't seem real either. I keep feeling as though they've all made some awful mistake and got the wrong person, Claire could still be alive and they've all accidentally switched the records over.

I know that's not the case as her Mum and Sister went to see her in the chapel of rest – but for me... there's a glimmer of hope.

That isn't the case I know that, but part of me hopes it is. I think when they return her rings to me that will be the final sign that it really was my beautiful Claire that it happened to.

Every day I write this I cry. I'm crying again now – 7am Saturday morning and I'm off.

So what part of me is holding on to the hope that it wasn't Claire?

The part of me that adored her?

The part of me that unconditionally trusted her?

The part of me that liked to cuddle her – yep that's the one... how do I know? Well, writing that set me off again so it must be!

I've not thought yet about what I will miss the most as that feels too negative, but to be honest the thing I'll really miss is holding her. Emotional, & practical support I can get from others, but her warm and friendly cuddle? Nothing can replace that.

I need to write a letter to her:

Claire,

I've not written anything to you yet, I've shouted a bit at home at you but not written. The kids have written each day on your Facebook wall, but me... I couldn't face writing to you until now.

Sweetheart, I love you so much. And right now I miss you so much. You were my world, and still are my world.

I drew my strength from seeing you each day and I only realise now how much strength you imparted simply by smiling at me.

I used to love our cuddles, the softness of your skin always reminded me of our first kiss back in '87 – yep, every time I held you I remembered that day – I don't think I ever told you that.

You were everything to me, no-one will ever know what a special relationship we had, only we could ever know that.

Do you remember that chat we had in the pub on the beach in West Bay last weekend? That was our last night out together and we talked about it being our new 'local' if we moved there. I remember almost every word of that conversation, it was deep – not some meaningless drivel but a conversation that really meant something. I loved our chats.

Thank you.

Thank you for the last 25 years together.

Thank you for ALWAYS being there.

Thank you for not judging.

Thank you for your kindness, gentleness and tenderness.

Right now at this moment I've run out of words. I've no idea how to finish this except with a huge (((((HUG))))) and a xxxxKISSxxxx.

Goodnight my sweetheart.

Tagged

- Funeral
- Hug
- Kiss

11. Day 11 Erasing The Past

After registering Claire's death on Friday and arranging the funeral I've now had to inform the authorities via the government's 'Tell Us Once' service. The registrar said it would be the quickest and easiest way to let libraries, passport, HMRC, DVLC etc know – and then to amend their records – and indeed it was easy, from a practical point of view at least.

It took me about 10 minutes to erase Claire from the 'system'.

It was horrible, it seemed as though with every page I clicked through to I was slowly erasing all traces of Claire – Passport, erased. Library card – erased. Drivers licence – erased.

Somehow it was TOO easy, you can't ERASE someone with a few clicks of the mouse – and yet in today's world that's what it has come down to.

Click – Gone.

I woke up this morning not feeling too bad, the girls slept in their own beds last night (they've been on blow up beds in my bedroom since Claire died), the sun is shining and it's a new day. Then I decided to do the government thing and it's not such a nice day anymore!

There's only one thing to do on days like this – tidy. And today the airing cupboard gets it!

Tagged

- Erasing

12. Day 12 A day of firsts

Each Sunday morning Claire and I used to have a Lavazza Latte made in our espresso machine – this Sunday was the first Sunday I've made only 1 coffee.

Last night I woke up cold in bed, it was the first night I've done that as we used to cuddle up to each other if we were cold.

Yesterday I cooked a Sunday roast, it was the first time I've ever cooked one and Claire not be there.

A day of firsts.

I know we are going to experience this a lot, especially during the first year as anniversaries, Christmas and birthdays come round – so I have a choice.

I can either dread each first and curl up in a corner, or I can become stronger knowing that we never have to go through that particular first again and we've overcome another small but significant challenge.

Claire was one of life's copers. She just got on with stuff and we often talked about the problems we encountered with the kids (those that know us well will know what we are talking about) – she always said to me:

"Mark, what can you change and what can't you change? Now only focus on changing what you can and accept the things you can't" – what great advice my sweet.

So I'm going to listen to Claire because she was always right, I'm choosing to live by her example with her as my inspiration – I can't change that she's gone, but I can change how I react to my 'day of firsts'.

Thank you my dear, you've inspired me once again. I love you.

Tagged

- *Coping*
- *Decisions*
- *Feeling cold*
- *Firsts*

13. Day 13 Is The Present Tense Right?

Last night was really tough. The kids didn't want Claire to be at the funeral in just a gown, they wanted her to be clothed in her own clothes and wearing her jewellery – so we spent the evening finding something appropriate that they were all happy with.

At the end of it, whilst it was just a pile of clothes, jewellery, her glasses and a watch, it seemed all too real. It seemed as though we had tried to reconstruct Claire in a very personal way.

The part I found the hardest was that each of the 4 kids have written a letter to their Mum that they want to read out at the funeral on Friday, they all made me cry. But what really made me cry was that they wanted a copy of those letters to go in the casket with Claire as their final notes to her, preferably clasped in her hands – oh man did I blub!

The one and only reason I'm writing this down is to resolve it in my mind. To articulate it and make sense of it.

It's not the loss of Claire that got me last night, it was the love that the kids were showing – a motherly love that can no longer be requited.

We talked about whether they should phrase their tribute in the past or present tense. "I loved my Mum" seems like it has stopped, and it hasn't.

We also realised that their mother is not the flesh and bones in that casket, Claire was more than that – she was WAY more than that – no really, Claire was way, way, way more than just flesh and bones – she truly touched our hearts.

And ALL that she was still IS and can never die – the present tense is absolutely right – they love her, she IS their Mum and she DOES live on in our hearts.

Tagged

- Love
- Mum

14. Day 14 Loneliness

Last night I realised that this is the longest time in 29 years that I haven't seen Claire. She died 2 weeks ago and the first year we were going out with each other, she was 15 and I was 16, our parents 'dragged' us on our family holiday for a fortnight and we didn't see each other – that's been the only time we were apart for this long.

We didn't live with each other before we were married, and so, since the 22nd June 1991 when we got back from our honeymoon we haven't spent more than 6 days apart and we've spoken everyday for those last 22 years.

Yes, I guess today I feel a little lonely.

Now here are my thoughts about loneliness:

Loneliness is a 'label' which has no definite meaning

Because it has no definite meaning it means different things to different people

Because it means different things to different people it can never be defined

Because it can not be defined, what is it anyway and does it even exist?

I can give how I feel a label, I can call it 'lonely' if I like but I won't let it define me. If I label myself as 'lonely' then people will feel a need to respond in a certain way... dependant upon THEIR idea of what that label means. If I label myself as lonely I might start acting that way even more, and so it will become a self fulfilling prophecy.

So I'm not 'lonely' I just want to talk to Claire. I want to hold her again.

What does holding her get for me?

I guess it helps me relax, feel warm inside, feel at peace. And if I close my eyes and take myself back to a time when I was holding her I can still feel that peace, relaxation and warmth.

Thank you Claire, you're still with me. I love you.

tagged

- Hug
- Loneliness
- Peace

15. Day 15 A Thank You

Over the past couple of days I've had a few conversations about coping and grief, and how we deal with those emotions. I know this website gets read a lot and so I want to say a public thank you to Bruce Farrow and Kim Blackmore plus Dr Tad James (although I've never met him!).

Almost 2 years a go I started a journey of personal development in understanding how we think, how we communicate and how we deal with emotions and manage our state. Bruce and Kim were the trainers on that journey.

As part of my development we undertook therapy for negative emotions using Time Line Therapy ® developed by Dr Tad James (hence the thank you to him also).

Over the past 2 weeks since Claire's untimely death the techniques, ideas and mind set I've developed have literally saved me from despair – each day I do Time Line Therapy on myself, learn from the day, apply what I learnt to myself, decide what I'll do differently next time and move on... just a tiny bit.

I'm experiencing one of the biggest significant emotional events it's possible to endure, yet I come to it clean. I have no baggage from the past which enables me to deal with this event, bit by bit, hour by hour and day by day. I deal with what I experience each day and resolve it.

Writing this blog helps as I can use it as a dialogue with myself, one sentence is often me being client, the next me being coach. It helps – enormously. So if you read these posts and it sounds like two people having a conversation, then that's often exactly what it is.

Bruce and Kim, I want to thank you from the bottom of my heart for giving me access to all my resources, for helping me realise that

I control my mind and therefore my results and for taking the lid off the dustbin!

Tagged

- Coping

16. Day 15 A sense of dread

Last night I experienced something really odd. A deep, painful and dark sense of complete and utter dread. If I think about my own death, about the eternity of not living I get that feeling, and last night, for the first time, I was thinking about Claire and all the lovely times we had and I got the same feeling. Deep, dark, black, heavy, in my chest rising and up & outwards down my arms.

A complete sense of dread. I'll never see, hear or hold Claire EVER again. Even writing that down seems to elicit that state in me again, and I can feel it rising in my chest...

So what if that deep and dark sense of dread that rises from my chest happened in my little toe... can I still feel it, can I get that old state back?

No.

Well I wouldn't want to do that then would I?

Each time I feel that deep and dark sense of dread that rises from my chest I'm going to force it in to my little toe, and for some weird reason I can no longer feel it.

This is weird shit, it works so I'm doing it.

The funeral is tomorrow. My little toe is going to get worked a lot.

Tagged

- Coping
- Dread
- Funeral

17. Week 3 Day 20 Moving on and grieving seems odd

I've not posted for a few days as we went down to Devon to spend some time with my sister and her family – thanks guys for having us – I must say I missed the therapy that writing this blog brings!

It was tough at the sea, being there without my Claire didn't seem right. Whenever we went we used to make a point of walking on the beach, hand in hand, often in the evening and talking about how nice it would be to live there – all a bit surreal.

We're settling in to some new routines which, to be honest, doesn't feel right. It feels as though we are re-writing our lives without someone who should be here.

On the one hand we need to move on and develop new routines, and on the other hand we need to... to.... to... I'm not sure what the words are. To respect, to grieve – yes that's the one – 'grieving' and 'moving on' seem at odds.

So what is the highest positive intention of grieving for me? Protection>love>peace>amazing joy.

And what is the highest positive intention of moving on me? Surviving>belonging>peace>amazing joy.

So actually, grieving and moving on have the same highest positive intention for me of 'amazing joy' – so I wonder if I could allow all the resources that are available to the part of me that wants to grieve, to share those resources with the part of me that wants to move on. Perhaps they could share those resources in synergy and harmony, working together for the same highest positive intention of allowing me to have 'amazing joy'.

Moving on and grieving have the same intention, so I can do both. It's OK to move on. It's OK to grieve. Their purpose is amazing joy. I can live with that!

Tagged

- Coping
- Grieving
- Moving on

18. Week 3 Day 21 Total recall

I really want to be thankful today, and most of all I want to be thankful for the vivid memories I have of Claire. Enjoying those memories is a great sign to me that I've come a long way in 3 weeks. Yep, it's 3 weeks today that Claire died.

Every now and then, when I was aware that I was enjoying a moment with Claire I made sure I fully associated in to that moment – it was a conscious decision to do and I have been doing it for about 5 years now.

As soon as I became aware that I was enjoying myself with her, it could be a chat, dinner, a romantic walk by the sea or simply she could have just looked lovely one day, when I noticed those times I made sure I didn't delete 'stuff' – I fully associated in to the moment to be aware of everything I possibly could.

I'd look around me and notice how she looked, what she was wearing, how she smelt, what she said, what words she used, what we were talking about, what noises were in the background, what the temperature was like, what I was wearing, if we were enjoying food/drink then what tastes was I experiencing, what were other people doing around us, how did I feel, where was that feeling, what was her hair like, what jewellery did she have on, what sensations was I experiencing, what was Claire's make-up like, what did her skin look like, how did it physically feel to hold her hand.

Noticing all those things deliberately means I REALLY enjoyed those times we shared, and what I didn't realise at the time was how easy it would be to recall those times when I can have no more of them.

My memories of those times are not some hazy distant memory, I have total recall. I can enjoy them over and over as if Claire was here.

And even though I'm crying again now at the thought of never doing that again, I am truly happy that I did what I did so I can continue to enjoy those moments with clarity. The name 'Claire' even means clear and bright. And she still is.

Tagged

- Memories

19. Week 4 Day 22 It means what I want it to mean and no more

Today I feel disconnected – like there's something important missing, the only way I can articulate it is to say I feel like I've had something amputated.

There's a part of me missing and it is the strangest sensation.

I don't really want to give the missing part of me a label as that will begin to lead how I feel, that part is clearly Claire but beyond that I simply can't articulate how I feel – and that's the first time I've come across that problem.

I think it's all tied up with the 'erasing' process. The other day my mobile rang and it was the home phone calling, so it popped up saying 'Claire is calling you' – that felt too weird so I had to delete her from my phone. Such a simple and actually meaningless task, yet I gave it meaning... OK – coaching mode kicking in now (I just spotted the complex equivalence trigger word in that sentence for any NLPers reading this), now I'm understanding it... I'm giving things meaning which don't have any meaning except in my head.

Deleting Claire from my phone doesn't mean anything, other than she's not in my phone.

Putting widower on an official form doesn't mean anything other than to tick a box for someone else.

Calling her 'my late wife' whilst on the phone to the pension companies doesn't mean anything other than a label that they can understand.

When I start out writing these posts I genuinely have no idea where they are going, I just type and see what happens and often in the middle I get a little light bulb go on and I reach a new understanding.

I understand now what I was doing, and I'm not doing it any more. It means what I want it to mean and no more!

Tagged

- Erasing
- Meaning
- Widower

20. Week 4 Day 23 Yesterday was a low day

Yesterday was a low day.

I thought that after the funeral all the nasty 'compulsory arranging stuff' would end and that we could get on with dealing with things – how wrong was I!

I've now got a huge pile of paperwork to complete, as with many couples we had no life insurance for Claire, but she worked for Barclays 20 years ago and more recently in the local school as a learning support assistant. Both Barclays and the school had pensions attached (tiny ones, but still something) that I can now claim.

As we have no debts, no credit cards, no HP and everything was in joint names I felt no need for a grant of probate, but these pension companies are insisting I have probate before they'll pay out... so now not only do I have to complete their lengthy forms, I have to go through the probate system as well. As if losing Claire and trying to find new routines to do everything she did around the house weren't enough, I now have this extra burden of form filling to claim pensions of £20/week!

Yesterday was a low day.

The loneliness is also starting to kick in. I know I'm not alone, but I really do feel lonely. Please don't ever take for granted your ability to 'share' with your partner, sharing is such a powerful and meaningful thing to do, even the small things like "Oh look that cloud looks like a duck" have a whole new meaning when you've no-one to share it with!

I used to store up little things like that to share with Claire for a few days and then we'd have a little chat over a coffee or on a walk – but now I can't and I feel so lonely.

Yesterday was a low day.

OK, so rather than wallow, what am I going to do differently next time that's positive, for me and that I can learn from?

30 MINUTES LATER

If you've not experienced Time Line Therapy® before you may not fully understand what this all means – apologies but this means a lot to me.

I've just noticed that my time line changed colour a few weeks ago, if I look to the past my time line is bright right up to Claire's death where it almost fades out, then if I turn to the future it still remains faded. I can change it in my mind but at the moment it's not easy to maintain.

Learning 1: Each day I must check my time line and ensure it's bright, if not make it as bright as I need to make it the brightest and most brilliant time line.

Looking down on yesterday what can I learn?

I feel like an island, alone and not connected. But as I go higher I notice something... what is an island surrounded by? Of course, it's a beach and the sea – even writing that down brings out the tears – Claire loved the sea, she felt alive by the sea, she wants to be laid to rest by the sea.

Learning 2: As that lonely island I am in fact surrounded by Claire. If I keep that picture in my mind, even though it makes me cry, I feel the love and warmth of her all around me.

Today will be a little brighter.

Tagged

- Coping
- Time Line Therapy

21. Week 4 Day 27 The journey to a new routine

Today I'm feeling rather overwhelmed.

Overwhelmed with a) The practicalities of running the house b) The practicalities of dealing with the legal side of Claire's death.

The legal side of things I'm happy to delegate to willing volunteers where possible, and indeed I have done, but the house side of things is different.

We need to work out the new routine of how we do things, and the answer lies in ourselves as a family. People have been REALLY kind and offered lots of help, and if there is a special event or similar (it's Toby and Theas' 16th and Olivia's 18th soon) I'm happy to accept help but for the everyday stuff we need to do it ourselves, we need our new routines.

Claire used to do the dog walk every morning and some evenings, now the kids have to do it.

The washing, cooking, cleaning, shopping, running about, arranging all now needs to be done by me – and on top of working it is a little overwhelming at the moment.

The only reason I'm writing this all down is to document how I feel NOW, so that in a few months I can look back and see how far I've come and how well we're coping.

Today is a marker of that journey, a conscious "This is my current destination" – because, just like a SatNav, if I don't know where I've started the journey can't be navigated. With my current location set I can see what needs to be done and plot my route to somewhere new.

There is a new routine out there for myself and the kids, we just need to complete the journey to find it.

Tagged

- Coping
- Over-Whelmed

22. Week 4 Day 28 Loss of Love

Whilst driving the other day I had a realisation. I'm not loved any more!

I'm not saying that no-one loves me, it's just that I'm not loved in a husband/wife way any more.

I had a long chat with 2 of the kids last night about Claire (To. and M.) – they too are feeling it... they aren't loved in a motherly way any more.

I guess we all feel that 'loss of love' in a different way, the love of a Sister, a Daughter, a Mum, a Wife or a Friend. And that love that's missing can never be replaced because it goes deeper than the specific role... it was the unique and special kind of love that Claire gave to her husband, children, sister and friends. And that love can never be replaced.

Life does feel empty without that love, it really does.

Coaching mode engage!

What does that love get for ME?

It's that sense of warmth, that spreads out and surrounds me, like putting on a really thick woolly jumper in the middle of a cold dark night.

That warmth of lying in a steaming hot bath and feeling the stress soak and relax away in to the water.

That warmth of a huge hug from the person you desperately love.

And once again as I think about it now, the picture of an island all alone and stranded comes to mind. Yet that same island is surrounded by the warm and relaxing sea that Claire loved so much.

I'm going to buy a big picture of an island and hang it on the wall, it'll remind me of that love each time I walk past it.

Love isn't something that emanates in a physical sense from another person, if it were then we wouldn't feel loved when they left the room. Love is something that endures in the absence of that person... so if that's true I am loved by a wife and the kids are loved by a mum – we just are!

Tagged

- Hug
- Loneliness
- Mum
- What is love
- Wife

23. Month 2 Week 5 Day 30 Missing Her

Yesterday I went to see a new client in Epsom, Surrey. On my way back I drove through Ashtead and remembered that my old boss that I worked for when I was 19 lived there... for some bizarre reason I could remember his address.

Via the joys of a SatNav I could see I was only 4 minutes away, I had no idea if he still lived there but I took the chance, knocked on his door and to my surprise there he was.

What a great 2 hours we spent catching up with our families.

Now the thing is this. I really enjoyed catching up with my old boss, he had a wayward son when I worked for him and I used to get stories of his exploits. He also had new born twin grandchildren, so again I used to get stories of all that twins get up to.

I used to come home and share all this fun stuff with Claire, and I know that if I'd been able to share what became of those kids and stories with Claire yesterday we'd have been talking for ages.

Yesterday I felt myself bursting with little stories to share with her. What the twins are doing now, what became of the wayward son, and more.

But I came home to nothing.

For the first time I had some stories to share and no-one to share them with. Even telling them to my Mum later last night wasn't the same as she didn't get all the original exploits 20 years ago. Claire did. Claire knows the full story and could have referred back to "do you remember the time when....".

I guess that's just part of what I need to let go of. She was the only person in the world that knew so much about me and my life which made those conversations so easy.

It's the interaction with Claire I miss. The deep, deep knowledge of understanding about every facet of our lives that being with someone for 28 years brings.

I've nothing more to add, other than I truly am missing her today.

Tagged

- Loneliness
- Missing her

24. Month 2 Week 5 Day 31 It's getting tough

They say 'It'll be tough' – so what is that 'it' that they talk about?
  It's getting tough now. But what is it?
  Can it be defined?
  Can we say what it is, or if it has gone.
  It's just a play on words isn't it, surely?
  And if it's just a play on words, we can't tell if it's gone and we don't know what it is... does it exist?
  I'm confused now about it. Good, it's gone!

Tagged

- Coping

25. Month 2 Week 5 Day 34 There's no fitting title

I'm really starting to notice that Claire shaped hole in my life now. She died just over a month ago and it really feels like it!

We're coping pretty well with the practical stuff, the kids are mucking in and our families have been great, it's the 'loss' stuff that is really hard to deal with.

I guess I've never really experienced loss quite like this before, most other emotions (it seems to me) we get a taste of throughout our lives – anger, fear, sadness etc we all get a little taste of – but loss we only ever experience when we're 'in' that situation fully.

When I wake up in the morning I feel it. In recent years (since I stopped needing to commute for an hour to work) Claire got up before me, so I'm used to waking up in an empty bed... but I used to look forward to coming down stairs and seeing her smile at me.

In the middle of the day, when I'm sitting in my office overlooking the road, I imagine seeing her car pull up outside when she comes home from work.

I used to look forward to her waving at me as she got out the car.

In the early evening, I often used to sit upstairs and watch telly and pop down to find Claire watching Coast or Escape to the Country or Homes Under the Hammer or some other seaside/property program – now I don't bother, I just sit in my bedroom thinking.

Of course I miss her all the time, but there are certain times of the day when it really digs, and living here, in this house, those old habits and constant reminders are prodding me almost every second of every day – and those prods are sharp and painful.

Where is this blog post going? I've no idea, but I needed to write that down so I am aware of when the feeling's gone... or at least reduced!

I watched 'The King's Speech' the other day – that was not nice. Claire and I wanted to see it at the cinema, but life overtook us and we never made it. We then decided we'd wait until the DVD came out and watch it then, but life overtook us and we never made it. We then thought we'd watch it on TV – it was on a few months ago and we recorded it, but life overtook us and we never made it.

I was then browsing the recorded programs and found it. It was really strange watching it without Claire – I mean, it's only a film but it just seemed wrong. Claire was supposed to be there as I watched it... just like she is supposed to smile at me in the morning, wave at me from the car and be watching Coast in the evening. But she wasn't and the sharp dig that I got still hurts.

Unfortunately with this post I can't think of anything positive to say, we just need time I guess!

===

POSTSCRIPT

On re-reading this I found a spelling mistake. I type pretty fast and most of the time I'm not thinking about which key to press, I'm thinking about the words to say. With that 'unconscious' typing I made a spelling mistake... or at least my unconscious typing made a mistake – and that mistake was in the first line. Instead of writing '...Claire shaped hole ...' I originally wrote '...Claire shaped whole ...' – perhaps my unconscious knows something I don't.

Today I'm going to let my unconscious mind notice what it needs to notice in order for that hole to be whole.

Tagged

- Loss

26. Month 2 Week 6 Day 36 Change Time

Up until now I've not really experienced such a significant single event, sure we've had some tough times (people that know us know what those are) but apart from when the twins were born and we nearly lost Toby things have been pretty stable – or at least they've seemed that way.

At the time things can seem up and down, like tracking the stock market up and down with one of those little charts they draw... up, down, up, down... almost a rhythm to it.

At the time it seems like it's up and down, but when we get a SIGNIFICANT event, like the death of a spouse and we pan out from that chart and take the whole thing in context, that small area of our lives seems to be constant when we can see that huge event in the context of everything else.

Up until last night I didn't realise how much my life has changed since 17th April 2013.

If I compare now to 16th April everything has changed – work, kids, home, relationship... everything!

That old life has gone – the routines, the way we did things, the habits, the aspirations, the plans – all changed.

Accepting that is difficult, but the reality is that there is no choice and Claire always told me "If you can't change it, accept it and move on to something you CAN change' – she was right... she always was!

Claire, it's the twins birthday today and we miss you. I remember 16 years ago when we almost lost Toby and he was hooked up to a ventilator looking really ill. You did so well, you were such a great Mum and you sat by them both for weeks in special care. It's days like today when we really notice you are absent. You are so missed, you really are. I love you so much Claire and this pain of loss is hard to take, but I know I have to get through it. Thank you for all you did sweetheart. We'll miss you today.

Tagged

- Acceptance
- Birthdays
- Change

27. Month 2 Week 6 Day 38 Wearing the armour part 1

This is so stupid.

Someone bought me a really nice bottle of red wine for my birthday (which was 2 days before Claire died) and I've not drunk it yet. When they gave it to me I thought "This will be nice to share with Claire one Friday night" as we often opened a bottle at that time.

I couldn't bring myself to open it before now, but tonight I did and I feel crap.

It's great wine but I feel lost and lonely with no-one to share it with. It's weird, when I shared a bottle of wine with my wife it felt special but when I drink it alone I feel like a craven alcoholic.

The only solace I can take is that this is the first time I've done it and I never have to go through it again.

28. Month 2 Week 6 Day 42 Wearing the armour part 2

The kids wanted to go to Blockbuster yesterday to rent a film, Claire was the only one that had a card so we had to look through her purse to find it. I still haven't done that yet, I've not sorted through any of her personal stuff, it's all exactly as she left it when she left the house on 17th April to go to the hospital. Her purse is in her bag which is hanging under the stairs, her pyjamas are in her bedside table and her clothes are piled up in her wardrobe.

Next weekend we have a family reunion with some Australian relatives, the following week is my eldest's 18th Birthday and the weekend after that would have been our 22nd wedding anniversary – I'm not clearing on those days, so I guess the job of clearing and sorting isn't going to happen for a few weeks yet.

The waking world can seem very dark and cold at the moment. I'm not in the depths of despair or anything like that, but I can see how it could be easy to go that way. It's like there is a bottomless hole opening up next to me, a hole that just goes down and down. Dark, cold and hard to climb out of.

There are days when I can look down into that hole and see it as the easy option.

It's tough staying above ground, it's tough fighting to stay on top. It's like when I'm out for a little jog, I reach the point when my body SCREAMS stop, and the easiest thing is to just give up and sit down.... but I could be a few miles from home so I have to go on and fight. The difference is that with this emotional battle is that there's no end point, no way of knowing when I can actually stop and rest.

I know the battle is entirely in my head, I know that in all of this the one thing I CAN control is what happens inside my head – I know I have the resources I need to firmly anchor myself to solid ground and keep from falling in to that hole.

It's unlike me to quote scripture, but this came to me this morning (after some Googling!)

"But since we belong to the day, we must be serious and put the armor of faith and love on our chests, and put on a helmet of the hope of salvation."

1 Thessalonians 5:8

That's exactly how I feel, like I must put on the armour for each day. And if that's what needs to be done, so be it.

29. Month 2 Week 7 Day 43 Each day I learn a little bit more

Yesterday seemed like a bit of a dark day, as you can probably tell from my blog post. It's strange how things can turn around quite quickly.

I'm doing what I can to keep fit now and regularly go out for a short jog, during the day yesterday it felt as though I was nearing the end of one of my jogs when my body shouts that it wants to stop. All I wanted to do yesterday was lay down and give up. When I went for a jog in the evening I started it with the same mental attitude and found after only 100 yards I was struggling. Every step I wanted to stop. It just wasn't happening.

But this morning I went out on that same jog along the same route, nothing has happened to me physically overnight but I went out with a different mental attitude today. I didn't focus on the pain of each step, I focused on the feeling of having completed 3 miles and how good that feels.

It is so true but when our eyes drop to focus on every step, we notice each one and how painful it is. Yet when we lift our heads, look to the future and keep going, things seem brighter and easier.

Each day I learn a little bit more.

Tagged

- Getting stronger

30. Month 2 Week 7 Day 44 What is grief?

I've been thinking a lot about this recently. I spend a lot of time online which is good from the point of view of finding out information, and bad because you never know if the information is good or not! We have a local hospice which offers grief counselling and bereavement support, the doctor made a referral for the family to them at the beginning of May, but typically for government organisations we've not heard anything yet!

Just so that I could connect with other people in a similar situation I've been browsing a few forums dedicated to grief and loss, particularly that of the loss of the spouse. They are a mixed bunch really.

One of the things that seems to be standing out is that everyone who is grieving struggles with the concept of what it actually is, and what they should do.

A person posted on one of the forums yesterday that her family thought she was obsessing about her late husband, she posted a whole host of things she was doing and asked the forum if she was indeed obsessive or whether this was normal.

The question is, what is normal? And who makes up the rules?

Reading through the posts that many of these people are making I've come to realise that in this situation we make up our own rules, and then beat ourselves up with them... What a crazy thing to do.

Each time I catch myself using words like should, must or ought I ask myself the question "Who says?" – and most of the time it's me, putting my own pressures on myself.

Learning to ignore myself is a strange thing to do. I'm learning to accept that however I feel at any given moment is absolutely fine, I don't have to do anything. There are no stages of grieving! People have said that everyone goes through seven stages starting with denial then anger then some other bullshit... Who says?

In my own grief I refuse to be defined by other people's version of normal. I refuse to define myself as a grieving person.

As ever I'm writing this post off the top of my head and things keep coming to mind, and what comes to mind now is the political correctness regarding disabilities (okay, my mind leaps around all over the place). I always used to think that the person with disabilities was 'disabled' – and I remember advertising campaigns saying they are not a disabled person, they are simply a person living with a disability. It always seemed like a semantic argument, but now I understand. I'm not a grieving person, I'm a person living with grief – I refuse to let it define me.

One of the other things that other people on the forums seem to struggle with is guilt. I can understand this but choose not to do it myself. Sitting here writing, if I think about it, I can find lots of things to be guilty about. Guilty that I didn't make Claire slow down a bit. Guilty that we didn't move to her beloved seaside a couple of years ago. Guilty that we didn't take her to the hospital sooner. But I choose not to beat myself up over these things. What's the point?

Guilt only serves one purpose and that is to destroy us. The reality is that Claire and I made the best decisions we could, at the time that we made them, knowing what we knew then. With the extra knowledge I have now, if I could go back in time, I would make different decisions. But when those decisions were made I didn't have that additional knowledge, and so we made the best decisions that we could.

I've let those things go.

One of the things that someone said on a forum yesterday was that people die, but love doesn't. I took comfort from those words which reminded me of what Claire and I have engraved on the inside of our wedding rings:

"Endless Love"

And it is...

Tagged

- Acceptance
- Grieving
- Love

31. Month 2 Week 7 Day 48 [no title]

I can't find the words to write at the moment. Nothing comes.

All that goes around my head is that when we had a major life crisis Claire used to cuddle up to me and say "Don't worry Markie, at least we've got each other".

Well now I haven't and I have to face it alone.

I thought I was as low as I could go, now I've no idea where the bottom is.

Tagged

· Feeling cold

32. Month 2 Week 8 Day 52 Keep looking up

I've got so much support around me from friends, family and work colleagues – thank you guys, you're all amazing and I really appreciate it.

There's no point to this post, I'm just writing how I feel because it's better that way.

When the party's finished, when the work is completed or when the day turns to evening everyone else's life continues the same as it did before with the familiar people around them. Mine doesn't. I come home to an empty house. I sleep in an empty bed. I've no-one to share the day with, no-one to say good night to, no-one to look forward to seeing first thing in the morning.

Waking in the mornings and the evenings are the worst times. They are so very quiet and I'm doing everything I can not to listen to the silence.

Silence really can be deafening.

There isn't anything anyone can do. In fact doing more things in the day (thank you to everyone that has invited me out or offered to help) in some strange way makes the silence worse. It's the contrast I think. Busy in the day and then BAM... it all stops when everyone goes home.

Sometimes it's just easier to keep things at a low level all day, then the evenings don't seem quite so bad.

Yes, I'm struggling, but YES I'm fighting too. I will win, I will learn to deal with the silence in some way and no matter how deep this black pit goes I will always keep looking upwards to I can see the light above me, no matter how far away it is.

Tagged

- Loneliness
- Silence

33. Month 2 Week 8 Day 55 Negatives don't attract

It was Olivia's, my eldest daughter's, 18th birthday on Saturday – that was a tough one. We went out for a meal as a family and yet at the same time we weren't a family. There was someone missing which left something missing from the room, something missing from the conversation and something missing in the atmosphere of the day.

Right at this moment in time every breath seems like an effort, the tiredness is almost overpowering, I make it to 8 PM each night and need to lie down.

Next weekend would have been our 22nd wedding anniversary and on reflection I think I can see where the tiredness is coming from.

It's almost as though I know I'm going to have to face these events, birthdays, anniversaries, Christmas and family celebrations without Claire. It's like these events have a magnet attached to them, except rather than be attracted to them I feel as though my body has the same negative polarity and I'm being pushed away. Those events are in the future and I'm being pushed to stay in the now and it's making moving forwards a hard slog.

Normally in life we have events to look forward to, those same birthdays, holidays and anniversaries are positive attractions. But without the one you love those days are to be avoided at all costs.

Right now I'm not sure what the solution is, I think finding something positive that I can look forward to would be good. The future would then hold some form of positive draw which would help to overcome the aching tiredness.

On an entirely different note I've had three people contact me via this website in the past week. Two of them have recently lost their spouse and one doesn't have long left as their partner is in the final stages of a terminal illness. One thing struck me, in times gone by I would have avoided any conversation that involved death. It's often a taboo subject and depressing to talk about. Yet not one of these three communications I had left me feeling depressed, in fact quite the opposite.

The conversation (via e-mail) with the person who is about to lose their partner to a terminal illness was the toughest, and yet even in what could be my darkest hours, it was good to help someone else. Knowing that my experiences, no matter how difficult they are to me as an individual, can help someone else can only be a positive thing.

50% of all couples will experience the death of their partner, I guess that is the reality, and so I know I am not alone!

So, back to work – Finding a new positive future is going to be my job this week. Something to look forward to, something that is a positive draw which can get me through the more challenging days... I wonder what that positive thing could be?

Tagged

- Anniversaries
- Birthdays
- Tiredness

34. Month 2 Week 9 Day 59 Happy to Wander

It would have been our wedding anniversary tomorrow – 22 years. I'm 45 now, so next year was the year when the balance turned to 50% of my life spent married to Claire. I was looking forward to that for some weird reason, being able to say "I've been with you for more than half my life" – and now the stark reality is that, if I live to a normal age of 75ish, I will have spent far more years without her than I did with her… and that hurts!

What has struck me over the past few days is how much I've changed. I've never really chased big money but what has happened has really focused my attention. Money, success, fancy cars, big houses count for nada. No I mean it, they count for NOTHING! Financial independence, financially free, passive income are all hollow terms that totally miss the point…

I received this from a dear friend recently who could be in financial trouble:

> "The last couple of months have been tough psychologically and now Claire's story has made me realise that I have nothing to complain about and just need to get on with things. Its amazing how we make some things important and then are given a lesson about priorities. I would go bust a thousand times for you if it would bring her back. So tell her "thank you" from me for making me realise what a fool I've been"

My life is refocusing on what really matters and if money, fancy cars and big houses happen as a result then I'm not going to turn them away, but I'm also not bothered if they don't.

Exactly what I want in life now is still unclear, Claire was my reason for everything I did and without that reason I admit to being lost – hence the name of this site! But for now, I'm happy to wander for a bit – in fact as I write those words 'happy to wander' they resonate with me and feel right.

Claire used to wander along the beach when ever we were there, just enjoying the air, kicking up the sand, digging around the rock-pools to see what's there, making something out of drift wood, chatting to the passersby and sharing the joys of the day with them.

For now, that seems like a good philosophy to adopt.

Tagged

· Change
· Focussed
· Wandering

35. Month 2 Week 9 Day 60 I made it through the day

"Happy wedding anniversary sweetheart"

I made it through today... our 22nd wedding anniversary. It's been an odd day, I've not really spoken to many people but those that I did, didn't mention that it was our anniversary. I guess it's tough for people, no-one really knows what to say, and I respect that.

I was having an SMS conversation with one friend who did indeed say happy anniversary in the message – and you know what I was OK with it, she knows about Claire and I'm actually very touched that she felt she could say that to me, it is my anniversary today and it always will be.

Of course it was a sad day, yes I've welled up quite a few times but it's not been a dark day... just sad, but acceptably sad... almost positive sad... is that possible?

I really am so thankful for the years we spent together, it's true that some people search a life time for what we had, and I am truly thankful that I found such amazing love and managed to share those 22 years with Claire.

Someone sent me this earlier on today – it sums up how I feel so well.

> The life that I have
> Is all that I have
> And the life that I have is yours.

    The love that I have
Of the life that I have
Is yours and yours and yours.
    A sleep I shall have
A rest I shall have
Yet death will be but a pause.
For the peace of my years
In the long green grass
Will be yours and yours and yours.

Tagged

- Anniversaries

36. Month 3 Week 9 Day 63 Roundabouts and Whirlwinds

This is more of an observation than anything else, but time seems to be passing so fast at the moment. No sooner have I woken up then it's time to go to bed again. The weekdays are blurring into one and the weekends seem to be hurtling by, one after another in quick succession.

I don't know why this could be, I guess it's a coping mechanism of some form?

There's no time to catch my breath, no time to sit and ponder – indeed, no time to really think about the impact of what has actually happened!

The only time I have experienced this in the past, albeit in a much milder form, is when we last moved house 11 years ago. I remember reaching agreement with the respective vendors and purchasers and making a phone call to the solicitor to start the legal process, from then on it was a whirlwind, a constant roundabout that we couldn't get off, and no sooner had the phone call to the solicitors been made then we were sitting outside the new property waiting for the removal van to arrive with our furniture to move us in.

It's that whirlwind roundabout that I seem to be on at the moment, except I'm not exactly sure which roundabout it is.

I'm rather hoping it doesn't complicate the issue but it looks as though our house sale is coming together as well – so I guess I'm going to be making that call to the solicitor pretty soon once more.

Another roundabout to step on.

Is it all too much?

Is there an answer to that question?

I'm really looking forward to moving house again, the new life by the sea, more relaxed, more chilled out, more space around us but without the very valuable immediate support of my parents and parents-in-law.

Just reflecting on that now reminds me of a recurring conversation that Claire and I used to have. We had often talked about moving to the sea and accepted the fact that it was possible that once we were there we could hate it. The conversation then always came round to us saying "We would rather live life and regret things we have done, rather than regret things that we haven't done and wished we did".

Claire my darling, you've come to my rescue once again, thank you.

Tagged

· Moving house
· Regret
· Whirlwind
· Roundabout

37. Month 3 Week 10 Day 66 The things I want to remember

Once again I'm not really sure what the purpose of this post is, memories lost, or memories retained.

I guess I have two options, the first is to complain about all the things I miss about Claire, except that would be a negative frame to look at it. In fact, those same things that I miss about Claire are the very things that I want to remember... And so here are those things that I never want to forget, and now they are down in writing I guess I never will.

- When life around us seemed like it was going wrong (and we went through a phase where some big shit happened) she would cuddle me late at night and say "At least we've got each other".
- The mock arguments we had. Claire wanted the tiniest camper van for some bizarre reason and when she spotted one would screech 'Oh, can we have that one? – we'd then have a silly & joking debate/argument with me telling her how silly she was.
- Her snoring that drove me to distraction, but oddly now the memory is a comfort as it's a sign she was alive.
- Her unfailing, unwavering and constant patience with the kids that surpassed my wildest comprehension. She truly did have the patience of a saint!
- Her intellect. She was one clever cookie.
- Our infrequent but long and deeeeeep conversations.

- The way she looked after me if I felt under the weather. "No, don't worry dear... I'll do it" was her stock phrase.
- The fact that she had a massive travellers chest FULL of recipes and we often joked that in 22 years of marriage she'd never cooked the same meal twice. If she cooked something different I would joke "mmm that was NICE, I'm looking forward to having it again when I'm 73".
- The love she had for Lowen our border terrier.
- Her get on and do it attitude. With the house moving project she'd arranged colleges and schools for the kids all well in advance.
- Her total ineptitude with anything that had a lock or key, especially the caravan where she once spent 20 minutes trying to get in, then drove all the way home to tell me the key wasn't working, I then drove to the van and opened it first time... she had the key upside down!
- Her incompetence with anything technological, especially mobile phones – a constant source of hilarity to both herself, the kids and me, especially when she tried to video Evie (our granddaughter) minutes after she was born, all we got was a video of Claire looking at the phone cursing "I've no idea how this stupid thing works, how do I turn it on to video?" – little did she know she'd already turned it on and we got the whole thing recorded!
- Her chocolate brownie cake at every birthday.
- Her complete love of the sea where she felt most alive.
- Seeing her hold and play with our beautiful grand-daughter Evie.
- Being there 5 years ago when we faced financial ruin and came close to losing everything. She planned, calculated the options and came up with alternatives whilst I found it hard to see the wood for the trees.
- Her giggles at the small things.

- Her uncontrollable crying at the big funny things that went on for ages.

Tagged

- Positive
- Sweet memories

38. Month 3 Week 10 Day 68 The Power of now

Sometimes the smallest things can get me thinking, and I never know where they are going to come from. It would be so easy to just give in to these negative thought patterns and spiral out of control, but there really must be a balance between listening to our body and getting on with daily life, if I completely listened to my body I'd curl up in a corner and not come out for quite some considerable time.

Someone asked me yesterday what my motivation for jogging was, they were saying how good they felt whilst exercising and that it is addictive. I must say, I feel no addiction to physical exercise at all... I never have. I don't get that endorphine kick and each workout is painful from the first step to the last; this is nothing new, it's always been that way with me.

I guess my motivation to get physically fit is that I now understand how fragile our grip is on this life. It'll never happen to me... 'It' always happens to someone else doesn't it? We watch programmes on TV about disasters and bad things that have happened in other people's lives... And there it is, other people's lives... It never happens to us does it?

Well, this time it did happen to us.

If I am a little fitter then my blood pressure will come down, not that it is worryingly high but it is higher than it really should be, my heart will be stronger and in the event that I do get ill I will be better able to fight it.

If something happens to me then the kids are completely alone, so there it is... That's what motivates me to jog.

So that thing that got me thinking what was 'it'? I was watching the news this morning and saw an interview with a tennis player who has recently finished his chemotherapy cancer treatment, I bet he never thought 'it' would happen to him, I bet he thought it always happens to someone else.

Our time on this planet is short, our time with the ones we love is often shorter and in this world of business planning, key performance indicators and business exit strategies I wonder how much this detracts from enjoying the now.

The only known is **now**. The only sure thing is **now**. The only guaranteed thing we can enjoy is **now**.

I wonder what we could notice if we simply spent more time enjoying **now**?

Tagged

- Enjoying
- Now (The Power of)

39. Month 3 Week 10 Day 71 All that I am I give to you

It looks like, in all probability, that we've sold our house.

This is the first major decision I've made without my beloved Claire and I'm left feeling really odd. And as I write that I've just had a epiphany as to why I feel odd... my reassurance strategy has an 'external auditory' that involves Claire, and of course that strategy can't run. If you're in to NLP you'll get that, if you're not then sorry but it makes sense to me!

On my to do list today, contact my coach and get that sorted!

So, back to moving house. Because I spent so many years living with Claire we became one, we acted as one and thought as one, consequently I'm not 100% sure that my decision to move down to the coast is completely mine. Losing a partner is not like losing someone external to yourself, it's as though an integral part of my body has been dissected out and I'm having to make life changing decisions on my own. I feel like an animal in a vivisection laboratory that has had part of his brain removed to see how it copes.

Every day living is fine, my business remains completely unaffected, both of which I'm very grateful for but when it comes to making life changing decisions, something isn't working quite right.

What strikes me is the uncertainty. When Claire was around we could bounce those uncertainties backwards and forwards and the process of doing that helped us make our minds up. Once I knew that Claire was happy with any decision, it was that that made my mind up for me. When I said those wedding vows just over 22 years ago I really meant it.

> I give you this ring
> as a sign of our marriage.
> With my body I honour you,
> all that I am I give to you,
> and all that I have I share with you,

All that I am I gave to her, and if she was happy I was genuinely and truly happy also.

Marriage requires that complete surrender to the other person, and when both parties do that it works. We did... and it did! But what when one partner dies? What then?

I guess it's a process of 'un-surrendering', of living with some uncertainty for a bit, enjoying it and seeing where it takes me.

Tagged

- marriage vows
- surrendering
- uncertainty

40. Month 3 Week 11 Day 76 The paradox of despair

I'm currently reading an excellent book called "Seven Choices – finding daylight after loss shatters your world" by Dr Elizabeth Harper Neeld. It's the account of Dr Neeld as she works through the emotions she feels after the loss of her husband to a very sudden death. Her story resonates deeply with my own situation.

Some of the things she writes are especially challenging and I'd like to share one of those challenging thoughts here.

Something which she has picked up on, which I strongly recognise, is the double loss of losing someone so close, not only have we lost the person as an individual but we have also lost our "Assumed Future". We all have an assumption about how our future will pan out, even if it is not explicitly written in a life goal (as mine was) we will have a general feeling or an idea about where life is taking us.

Visits to the park, Christmases shared, birthdays celebrated together and even things further off – we imagine growing old, how life will be once our own children have grown up and the time we can share with each other in the future.

I'm not just talking about myself here, I'm talking about Claire's sister, brother, mum, dad and my own kids. We all had an assumption about how life could possibly be in the future and we now have to face the loss of that as well as the loss of Claire herself. In fact anyone that knew Claire would also have had these assumptions about the future and how they would share their lives together in years to come.

This deep loss leads us to a place of despair. Despair is a word, indeed an emotion which I have never considered before. Of course I knew what the word meant academically, but now I know what it means to experience it myself.

As Dr Neeld points out, and this takes some deep thought, the fact that we are experiencing this despair means that our assumptions have been destroyed, and when assumptions are destroyed it opens up enormous possibilities. Wow, what a paradox!

When I did my creativity module of my MBA we spent many months looking at how assumptions by people in business stifle creativity and how breaking down those assumptions about their 'given future' in their career would massively help the business and greatly improve creativity. Without assumptions all we are left with is possibilities.

And there is the irony!

The truth is that if we feel that despair then we also have a world of possibilities. The challenge now is to allow those possibilities to happen at the same time as giving despair the respect it deserves.

Claire. My head knows that this is the truth and this is the kind of discussion I truly miss. Ironically, we could have spent a couple of hours discussing this and I know in my heart that you would have come to the same conclusion. You would have recognised the paradox of despair and possibility, indeed with your counselling training you may already have done so. I'm not going to lie, my heart feels differently. All I can feel at the moment is despair, I know the possibilites are out there and I guess that the first stage is recognising that – accepting and looking for those possibilities is something I can work towards. Goodnight sweetheart, I love you.

Tagged

- Despair
- Future
- Plans
- Possibility

41. Month 3 Week 12 Day 83 A new chapter by the sea

We went down to our new house over the weekend to have a chat with the guy selling it. Nothing is definite yet as we haven't exchanged contracts, but as far as we are able to tell everything is good and we should be moving there late August or early September.

The house is in a small village in West Dorset and is about 0.8 of a mile from the beach. Claire informed me that we had been to the beach a few years ago, but I must say that with my man memory I have no recollection, and so I decided that we'd walk to the beach on Saturday to see how far it was from our new house to be.

We set off walking from the house and just 20 minutes later Thea, Millie, Toby, Olivia, Tommy (O's boyfriend), Evie and myself were on the beach.

I was overwhelmed with emotion, both good and bad at the same time. It felt great knowing that we would probably be living a short distance from such a fantastic beach which we can visit at any time but at the same time it was so sad knowing that this was Claire's dream, and she came so close to realising it herself.

Claire desperately wanted to live by the sea and we often spoke about when we eventually would. She saw our new house about a week before she died, so at least she died knowing that she would be moving to the coast fairly soon. It just makes me sad to think that she never actually made it.

Losing Claire has changed me so much. I can't put my finger on what it is exactly and the only way I can describe it is as a "bollocks, I'm doing it" attitude! Facing mortality and death like this is bound to change our beliefs and values in our own life – and I think this is where the problem lay for people that don't deal with their grief. The shift in our thinking changes so much that it becomes difficult to cope with.

Facing these issues head-on has become really important to me, I know that it would be easy to store up many negative emotions because it's so difficult to deal with all of this change in thinking which has happened so fast. All that I know is that this is a process which happens slowly over time, each day we deal with a different issue and we move on. How long the process will take I have no idea and in fact I'm not going to focus on that at all. The problem is that we have no way of knowing that the process is finished and so why even bother asking ourselves the question, 'is it finished yet?'.

If I'm working as a coach with a client that wants to be more confident or happy I will always ask them "How do you know that you are as confident or happy as you want to be, what will you see, hear and feel specifically?" – using this same logic on my own grief leads me to ask the question "How will you know that the grieving process has finished? What will you see, hear and feel specifically?" – unless I can answer that question with absolute clarity there is no point in me wondering how long will this will take because without clarity around that question I could end up feeling low for ever.

Moving house won't sort all of this out I know that. But we started the process together as a couple, we were about to begin a new chapter in our lives and I'm looking forward to beginning a new chapter albeit in a rather different way to how I originally expected.

Tagged

- Coping
- Moving House
- Grieving
- Moving on

42. Month 3 Week 12 Day 85 My Beautiful Daughter's Prom

Last night was my beautiful daughter's prom. It was tough.

The kids all met at a friends house for a pre-prom party, so many Mums were there having their photographs taken with their kids, a tough day.

It wasn't easy for me to get there yesterday and I now know the full horror of what being a single parent is actually like. I'm trying to work a full day, look after the house, keep everything running and be there for the kids at the times when they need me. Thea told me that I didn't need to worry about going to the pre-prom party and I almost didn't go, but I moved some things around working a little later in the evening and I'm really glad I did.

The temptation to say "Claire would have loved this" or "It's so sad that Claire isn't around to see this" is mightily strong, but doesn't get us anywhere. I could go on and on, all day every day thinking the same thing. Every new experience is something that Claire is missing out on. She won't get to see her kids grow up, get married or have more children of their own. She won't get to live by the sea or enjoy all of that time we had planned travelling around in a motorhome visiting the coast of the UK.

I'm not sad for myself, I'm sad for her.

The love that she had for us endures yet so does the pain of her not sharing these experiences with us.

This has been the hardest post to write for some time, I guess it's because yesterday was such a 'real' experience made more noticeable by the presence of all the other Mums.

I'm not sure yet of the best way to cope with this kind of loss. The loss of those shared experiences, those experiences that we would have enjoyed together that now have been tainted with loss. I suppose one of the ways of coping is to just avoid those experiences, never to have fun again! I can certainly see why that would be appealing for some people, if we have lost someone dear to us and we just curl up into a ball then we won't have any positive experiences which make the pain of loss feel greater.

Every time there is a positive experience we are reminded that we are not sharing it with the one we love. And that hurts.

But I'm not going to do that, I'm going to put myself in a position where I can have those positive experiences and when I'm reminded that I'm not sharing them with Claire I will experience the loss, the sadness and the hurt that she is not there with me – I will acknowledge those feelings, I will learn something from those feelings, I will apply what I learn to myself so that next time I experience it I can grow – and then I will move on.

And for me, that's the way it has to be...

Tagged

- Coping
- Loss
- Prom
- Single Parent

43. Month 3 Week 13 Day 90 Removing a Critical Component

My middle daughter (16 years old) wanted to go to the shops on Saturday and asked if I would go with her, oh joy I thought!

We wandered around for a bit going in and out of various shops whilst she looked for the sunglasses she wanted and I really noticed how sorely lacking in certain skills I am. The whole 'shopping' thing is totally beyond me, I do man shopping and it takes me a few minutes to get what I want and then I'm in the car and going home again.

It just highlights the things that Claire used to do which we all took for granted. Don't get me wrong, Claire hated shopping too and we often joked that she could be an honorary man when it came to her style of shopping, but at least when the girls wanted someone to accompany them, she knew how to play the good mother and join in the 'fun'.

It's also been a few family members' birthdays this week, and I missed them. Once again, I'm a typical man.

If things were the other way round and it was me that had died then Claire would be writing the same things I'm sure, from a different perspective. I suppose it's to be expected that as we get back to normal, what ever normal is, we begin to notice the old 'normal' things that are difficult or impossible to do now.

I'm quite resourceful person so can usually cope in most situations, but it's so difficult when I spent 22 years not exercising a whole load of resources. It sounds sexist but there are whole load of 'motherly/womanly' resources which Clare had in abundance and so it was easier to let her look after that side of things in life. And now I can almost see the gaping hole where those resources should be, but I don't even know what they are let alone how to begin using them.

Sending birthday cards, booking holidays or going to the shops with the girls sound like easy things to do, but I'm struggling to know where to start.

Making the printer work, packing the car to go on holiday and finding the best deal to shop online is what I know how to do and to me those things seem easy, but ask me to get organised enough to buy a birthday card a week in advance, write it and get it to the post box and I'll struggle. I just haven't used 'that resource' (what ever that resource is) for 20 odd years.

I guess that's one of the problems of working together in a marriage, like a well oiled and highly efficient machine, as soon as one of the critical components is removed the whole machine falls apart – Our marriage worked so well because we worked so well together, and it seems ironic that it is that very fact that makes things so tough now.

I know that as time goes on I will recognise what resources are lacking and begin to find out how to use them but in the meantime if I miss your birthday please accept my apologies.

Tagged

- Birthdays
- Man stuff
- Resourceful
- Woman Stuff

44. Month 3 Week 13 Day 91 A weird thing keeps happening

When I started writing this site about my journey of coping with grief my intention was to use it like a permanent diary so that I could chart my progress over the years to come. This post is one of those.

I keep experiencing this weird existential feeling, a live 'as it happens' dissociated viewpoint where I am aware of what I am doing and can see everything through my own eyes yet I have a concurrent sense of viewing myself externally.

It's kind of like being aware of two peoples' viewpoints of the same situation at the same time.

I quite often experience this when I am presenting or running a course. I can be in mid-flow, delivering some excellent content (at least that's what I believe!) with passion and enthusiasm and yet at the same time I can see myself doing it and my brain is in a different place thinking about what I'm going to say next.

From what I remember I've spoken to other people that do public speaking and they say they have had similar experiences whilst delivering a presentation or course, so I guess that is not so uncommon.

I've never experienced this in any other situation though, but recently it's happened a few times whilst I have been going about my everyday business. It normally happens when the house is quiet, perhaps first thing in the morning or last thing at night. I become aware of myself making breakfast and at the same time can see myself making breakfast wondering where Claire is and is this all genuinely real?

To make sense of it I'm going to take a stab at understanding why it's happening...

...OK, so it's now 20 min later, I wrote a few paragraphs about why I think it is happening and gave up. They were gibberish.

I think what I can learn from writing this post is that experiences perhaps don't always have a reason – they just happen. I think we can sometimes over analyse why we do things or what is happening in a desperate human attempt to create order out of chaos. And now strangely I'm reminded of when I studied chaos theory in my MBA, isn't it odd how things come to mind and can be triggered by one word?

What I clearly remember from looking at Chaos Theory is that it can look very much like chaos and yet at the same time be self ordering and self-sustaining. I'm reminded of an example that was given to us of an empty beach. If we allowed people slowly onto the beach, one by one, it would be completely chaotic as to where people sat. And yet people would end up all sitting an equal distance from one another. The chaotic system of arranging where we sit on the beach is in actual fact self ordering.

So my lesson today is to let the chaos happen, know that the chaos is actually self ordering and relax without any explanation of why it happens... It just does!

Tagged

- Chaos
- Dissociated
- Existential

45. Month 4 Week 14 Day 93 Goodbye Old, Hello New

So many people are sending messages and e-mails in response to my blog posts, thank you, please keep them coming you are not bothering me, you are not annoying and it genuinely helps.

Each time someone responds I have a new realisation, and here is one of those.

Here is a snippet of what was sent to me yesterday:

> I realised that the loss of <name removed> had changed me forever, and importantly I realised that this was OK.

I know that I have changed, and with my training as a coach I recognise that my beliefs, values and decisions have all been jumbled up, reordered and have yet to settle.

I also realise that it is okay to change. It's acceptable for me to reorder my beliefs, values and decisions to become a new person.

The battle I'm having at the moment is that I don't want to! I put a lot of effort into my life up until 17 April 2013, a considerable amount of hard work went into my business, my personal life and especially my relationship. That hard work grounded my values and beliefs and ensured that they were all aligned to achieve the same goal. I was happy with that, it felt right and everything with the world was good.

All that has changed now, my beliefs and values have changed immeasurably and it's so hard to let go of the way things were because of the hard work that I put into all that. And the truth is

I don't really want to let go but similarly I guess I need to as a key component of all of that i.e. Claire is now missing.

If you are happy in your relationship with your partner imagine being told that you have to abandon all of that, completely walk away and change everything. You would be pretty loathe to do so wouldn't you, and understandably so. Yet that is how I feel. On the one hand Claire is here with us, and if she is then I want to keep hold of that. On the other hand Claire has gone, and I need to let go.

You see my problem?

I need to make a decision to let go of the old me and welcome the new me, soon.

Tagged

- Moving on

46. Month 4 Week 14 Day 97 An empty wardrobe

This weekend has been the toughest by far for two reasons, firstly we sorted through Claire's clothes on Saturday and yesterday I sorted through the loft and found a load of diaries.

Sorting through the clothes wasn't actually as bad as I thought it would be whilst we were doing it, but it all hit me afterwards when everything was quiet and I was sat in my room with an empty wardrobe. That wardrobe feels like a metaphor for my life at the moment. There was a compartment in my life that was filled so completely, wholely and perfectly by Claire and just as that wardrobe is now empty, bare and actually completely pointless unless it is filled so it is with that compartment in my life – bare, empty and pointless.

We also found some diaries that Claire wrote for the kids. I was amazed to discover that she wrote a pregnancy diary for all four children charting how she felt every single day of the pregnancy. She then also kept a new baby diary, again charting how she felt every single day for the first few months of each of our children's lives.

I didn't know she did that.

I just want to hug her and thank her. She has left us a memory of how she felt, a memory that would otherwise have died on the 17th April when she did.

I miss her too much and can't write any more today.

Tagged

- Missing her
- Clothes

47. Month 4 Week 16 Day 109 Willing to Consider

You may remember me talking about an excellent book I'm reading called "Seven Choices" [1], it really is helping enormously. Up until Thursday of last week I was struggling with the concept of letting go. Why would I want to let go of something which was so perfect? The idea of letting go of the relationship that Claire and I had was not something I was even willing to consider, until I read the most recent chapter in Seven Choices.

I have realised that I don't need to let go of anything at the moment, of course in time I need to readjust to a new way of life but all I need to do at the moment is to be willing to consider this new way of life. That's the first step, just a willingness to consider things. The book also talks about incorporating my loss into this new life. That was also something I hadn't considered before, I was just imagining that the past was the past, it was done with and we move on.

That was too painful to even consider and so the idea of working with the loss, incorporating the loss somehow into my life feels much more acceptable and doable. I can indeed be willing to consider a new way of life which incorporates the loss, that feels so much better than the idea of letting go.

Exactly what that means practically I'm not sure yet. My next step is to begin to work out what that new life will look like, and to take active steps towards achieving it. New routines and new plans will allow me to continue life and live it to its maximum, all the while incorporating the loss of Clare into it. Not ignoring the loss, but working with it. It won't go away, how can it? It's happened and that can't be undone but I can forge a new life building the loss of Clare into it.

If I had to put some kind of scale to it with 0 being at the beginning of the process and 10 being complete, then I'd put myself at about 0.25 at the moment. I've just begun. The pain is still immensely raw. Every night, and I literally mean every night, I look to the empty side of the bed and am reminded of what I've lost. In fact I am reminded of what I've lost every waking second as I walk around this house.

But I am willing to consider the possibility of a new life. Just being willing is a start and something to build on, and build on it I shall.

[1] "Seven Choices" – Elizabeth Harper Neeld PH.D, Grand Central Publishing, ISBN 978-0-446-69050-8

Tagged

- Letting go
- Possibility
- Willingness

48. Month 4 Week 16 Day 111 Which way to look – a bouncy existence

Sometimes it's difficult to know which way to look.

Looking forwards is **positive.**

Looking forwards gives me the opportunity to create a brand-new future, to have complete control over what I do and to take things in a different direction.

Looking forwards is **negative**.

Looking forwards brings about a sense of anxiety and stress, how do I cope with everything that needs doing without Claire?

Looking backwards is **positive**.

Looking backwards gives me the opportunity to be thankful for the 28 years that Claire and I spent together, being married for 22 of them. Such happy memories.

Looking backwards is **negative**.

Looking backwards brings a sense of longing and reminds me of everything that I've lost.

And all that leads to a rather bouncy state of mind, bouncing backwards and forwards from positive to negative. The bouncing can happen quite quickly from the tiniest of triggers which can never be predetermined. The other day I was watching a TV programme, I can't remember what it was but I can remember I was enjoying it. I felt positive. And then all of a sudden I realised that I could never enjoy a TV programme again and share that enjoyment with Claire. I felt negative.

I'm excited about moving house and looking forwards to a new life by the sea, I feel positive. Which reminds me of the life I'm leaving behind and everything that Claire knew, I feel negative.

This bouncing of emotions seems to be common amongst the grieving from what I can tell, which makes keeping up our relationships with friends and family pretty difficult at times. One minute I want to see people and the next minute I want to be alone – almost as capricious as the British weather, and certainly as unpredictable!

So if you know anyone that has recently lost someone close to them, bear with them. If they want to see you one-minute and don't the next then it's just them coming to terms with the loss.

I know that what I need to do is to make those positive views as bright and close and vivid as possible, all the while turning down those negative views to make them as dim, faraway and still as possible. If I change how I see those views of forwards and backwards and decide to make them bright or dim then I control how much of an impact they have. So whilst I can't control the events themselves I can control their impact, and therein lies my little revelation for today...

Tagged

- Bouncing
- Negative
- Positive

49. Month 4 Week 17 Day 113 Grief "I just sit"

[PostScript added after I wrote this, please bear in mind as you read: I'm not going to kill myself so don't worry, it's just better that I write down truthfully how I feel rather than try and hide it in the hope that it helps not only myself but other people in the same situation as me]

This is a rather odd post and it comes as the result of checking the words that people type in Google when they end up on this website. It seems lots of people are typing Grief "I just sit" – and ending up on my site, of course I don't know why they typed that but I know where they are coming from.

The temptation to just sit and do nothing often reaches the point of being unbearable. I often feel like one of those deep cave explorers, sitting on the edge of an enormous black chasm, dangling my feet in, looking down and wondering what it's like down there in the depths. Except the depths of this chasm are the depths of depression... And it's very black down there.

The grief can often hit me in waves and sometimes all I can do is just sit. But when I sit I know that my feet are dangling on the edge of the chasm and I could easily fall in.

The strange thing is that I was always terrified of death, but now with Claire passing so early in life it seems that if she can do it then it can't be that bad. Dying doesn't seem so bad any more and just writing that down strikes me as being odd, but I don't care. This change in the way I view dying could make it seem like an easy option, an easy way to get rid of the pain.

I'm not contemplating killing myself or anything like that all I'm saying is that I can now understand the full process that could lead to it.

So how do I get up when all I want to do is sit?

One of the most liberating concepts that I adopt is the idea of choice.

If I want to get extremely angry then I can, it's a choice.

If I want to shout and bellow and curse then I can, it's a choice.

If I want to feel successful then I can, it's a choice.

If I want to feel happy then I can, it's a choice.

Once we truly accept that the way we feel is always a choice then we can choose to wallow in our own sadness or depression for a bit, but I can also choose to step out that sadness and depression. It's a choice.

Now it may not be an easy choice, we may not have access to all of the resources we need in order to make that choice at that given moment, but those resources are there buried within us – all we have to do is look hard enough.

So sometimes I choose to just sit, and then I choose to get back up again. It's MY choice.

Tagged

· Choice
· Grieving

50. Month 4 Week 17 Day 114 Life as a book

"For a long time it had seemed to me that life was about to begin – real life. But there was always some obstacle in the way, something to be got through first, some unfinished business, time to be served, a debt to be paid. Then life would begin. At last it dawned on me that these obstacles were my life."

Alfred D'Souza

I read those words yesterday and they hit home, they hit home pretty hard.

I enjoyed lunch yesterday with a good friend (thanks Emma) and we were talking about the 'when/then' game. When the kids have left home then it would be better. When I've moved house then I can relax. When/then.

Claire and I used to joke that we would write a book called "It'll be better when..." and then make jokes about all of the times that we had used that expression or heard other people use it, perhaps that's a project of the future, but thinking about it now really does make me stop and consider things.

What has opened up for me now is a completely new chapter in my life, I thought I knew where the story was going until I turned the page on 17 April and the great author in the sky decided to take the story in a different direction. I can see now that those early chapters were leading me in a direction and I had made up my own ending, I was pinning all of my hopes on chapters I was yet to read, life was going to begin in those chapters.

But as I sit here writing this down I can see the entire book, it's closed so I've no idea where the story goes, but I can see that this IS my life. It doesn't begin over the page, it began at the beginning of the book and I'm in it now, this is it, these obstacles ARE my life.

There is a lot to be said for writing the end of the book ourselves and creating our future as we go, and there is also a lot to be said for reading the words of the page that we are on, reading them slowly, reading them with meaning and most of all enjoying them.

I've no idea what is over the page, at the moment I have no idea what the next paragraph says, but I do know that for the time being at least, I'm going to read those words very slowly.

Tagged

- Acceptance
- Decisions
- Meaning
- Possibility

51. Month 4 Week 17 Day 115 Reasons and excuses

Since Claire died I've been making more of an effort to keep fit and because I'm too tight to go to the gym I've taken up jogging. I hate it! Every step is hard work and I don't get that 'kick' out of physical exercise that so many seem to report, I just find it a real chore but I know that it's all down to me now to look after the kids and so I have to stay in as good a shape as possible.

Every time I go for a run I'm looking for an excuse not to go.

Every time I go for a run I find an excuse.

When I'm actually out there running the only thing I ever think about is Claire, she dominates my thoughts from the first step to the last which makes the whole jogging process even more painful – and I'm not really keen on putting myself through unnecessary pain. But last night I realised something for the first time.

Losing Claire is my reason to go jogging. Losing Claire is my excuse not to go jogging.

It would be so easy to use this almost intolerable time as an excuse to not do anything. To lay down in the corner and not get up again. But if I change my viewpoint for a moment I can see that it's actually a reason to go on.

=========OK, now I'm crying again – you have no idea how much therapy I get from writing this =========

Up until this very moment I thought I'd lost my reason for living, I thought I did everything for Claire and that with her gone I had no purpose. She was always my reason for working so hard, building the business and even getting up in the morning.

But I was using that reason as an excuse not to think about the future and what it holds.

But now I can see that reasons and excuses are so close to each other and all that is required is a slight change in viewpoint and I can see that she is still my reason. Up until this very second I have actively avoided thinking about the future, it was an excuse. So as I take a different viewpoint now I find that I can take the old reason and turn it into a new reason to rebuild, and that for me is life changing today!

Tagged

- Decisions
- Excuses
- Reasons

52. Month 4 Week 17 Day 118 Two pictures

Picture 1

Life is a real battle at the moment. It seems as though every day has a series of hurdles to overcome and each day I feel like I'm running 100 m through the thickest treacle imaginable.

It seems as though the treacle just keeps getting thicker and thicker, it's relentless and getting deeper everyday. Just a great big sea of treacle.

I wonder when it will end. I can see the treacle horizon but the sea just seems to go on and on. I remember discussing with Claire once the idea of going on a cruise, she wasn't keen because she didn't like the idea of not being able to see the land. She told me that she could imagine being out in the middle of the ocean with no land in sight, only the watery horizon to look at and when she thought of that she got a rising sense of panic.

That's how I feel now.

If I could see an island in the distance then it would spur me on, I'd get a sense that the end was in sight and an idea of how much longer I needed to keep going for, but the way it is now I keep wading and it just keeps going.

I think what I'm looking for is an end to the pain of the way I feel now. I'm looking for the light at the end of the tunnel or a glimpse of an island of respite appearing on the treacle horizon, but I'm not sure that that is a particularly healthy viewpoint to have.

I want the way I feel to stop, but the way I feel is related to the loss and by its very nature that loss can never be regained.

It's so easy to give loss a meaning that it doesn't have. To give it attributes like treacle, like the sea, like a tunnel with no end. But that's not true is it? That's only the way I am choosing to view it.

So reflecting on this now I can choose to view it a different way so let's try this, let me start writing this update again with a different analogy.

Picture 2

Life is a real battle at the moment. It seems as though every day has a series of hurdles to overcome and each day is getting easier.

All I feel at the moment is a deep red mist of uncertainty. The redness is a deep blood red painted along the wall of the corridor next to me, but as I go through each day the deep red that seems so overbearing at the moment begins to fade.

Each day, with less red paint to put on the wall, the intensity gets less. I can see that overtime that deep blood red turns to a soft pink and if I look down the entire corridor, whilst the redness is always there, at the end of the corridor it fades to a gentle rose tinted white. The redness never goes but it turns from something overbearing into something that is actually quite beautiful.

I wonder if the memory of Claire which leaves me in so much pain at the moment can also be turned into something beautiful in the future?

I wonder...

Tagged

- Coping

53. Month 4 Week 18 Day 121 Press the button and change your plans

So many wonderful people have sent me messages recently, this one particularly got me thinking:

> "...you are really excited about your vacation to Italy, you plan, map out and are all set for a fantastic vacation. You board the plane with your plans, maps, highlighted spots to visit, etc. and you land in Holland. What happens then?...do you embrace the beauty of Holland and all that Holland has to offer or do you just focus on Italy and what your plans were?"

Claire and I really did have plans, we were going to each work two or three days a week and spend the rest of the time bimbling around in our camper van. When our youngest child was 18 Clare was also going to have a sabbatical, anyone that knew her knows that she could tell you exactly the number of years, months and days until that was. Claire TOLD me, yes TOLD me that she was going to have an entire year where she did no cooking, no cleaning and no looking after anyone else and that we would have to spend that year running around after her. Fair enough I suppose after all she had given up for her family.

From my perspective I have been ensuring that my business is mobile and can be run from anywhere in the country leaving us free to travel and me able to do a few hours of work each day from where ever we parked the campervan.

That plan went out of the window on 17th April this year.

There must be something in our human nature which upsets us if our carefully laid plans don't work out. What happens if we board the plane to Italy and land in Holland?

I saw a video recently from Heineken, listen to the reasons people give for not being able to change their plans.

[watch the video here https://youtu.be/RuiPbD72Kp8 or search "Heineken Departure Roulette HeinekenUSA" on Youtube]

"There's no way we can change these plans, this is a bachelor party"

"I'd have to go through security and get on a plane and then go back to my real life"

"I can't cancel this trip because it's for work"

I find it striking watching that video and seeing the similarities in my life at the moment. The anxiety about pressing the button, 'I can't do it, I've got plans' is exactly how I feel... 'Claire can't die now, we've got plans'

But the button has been pressed, someone pressed it for me and took the decision out of my hands, I'm in a destination that I've never even heard of let alone considered visiting, and so I guess it's down to me to make the most of it, right?

Tagged

- Plans

54. Month 5 Week 18 Day 126 Is it a dream?

It still feels like this is a dream, like its happening to someone else, almost a complete existential experience somewhat like those dreams where you think you are dreaming, but aren't quite sure and then wake up with a start and are grateful that what you just experienced wasn't actually the truth.

I'm still living in a vague hope that this is actually a dream, I'm sure it's part of the coping process that my unconscious mind allows me to believe that I might wake up. So in that sense I'm grateful for the protection.

My biggest challenge at the moment is working out what I want from life again. When Claire was alive I knew exactly what I wanted, I knew how many days a week we wanted to work, I knew what we wanted to do with our time off, I knew where we wanted to live and to support all of that I knew how much revenue I needed to be generating from my business, how I would go about doing that and what the profit would be in order to support what we wanted to do. Oh yes, I knew what I wanted.

Take Claire out of the equation and the entire thing falls apart. Claire was the WHY in my life, which gave me a clear sense of the WHAT I needed to do, all I did then was work out the HOW. Take away the 'why' and suddenly there's no reason for the 'what'.

Whether this is the actual truth or not doesn't matter, what matters is that it is my truth.

I've spoken to a good friend who is trained in the same coaching style as me, she wants some coaching too and so we have agreed to beat each other up, sorry I mean coach each other for a couple of days in October (thanks Emma).

I'm really looking forward to it, I'm apprehensive at the same time but I know I need to rebuild my future taking everything that was good and create a new life. At this moment in time I know that the beliefs I held to be true have been shattered and the things I valued in life have changed incomprehensibly, Emma you have an enormous task ahead of you as you put me back together!

On the one hand I want to keep that old goal, Claire and I had spent 22 years working on it, like an exquisite oil painting of our lives together. But on the other hand I've lost the artist that helped me paint that picture, however what I can do is look at that picture and take everything that was good about it and use that learning to paint a new one.

Tagged

- Coping
- Positive

55. Month 5 Week 19 Day 128 I'm living on the edge

I've heard people say " I'm on the edge..." before, but I never really knew what it meant.

I do now.

I get to the end of the day and I am shattered, the sheer mental and physical energy that is required to stay away from the edge is unbelievable. I'm on the edge of collapsing in a heap every second. I'm on the edge of breaking down every second. I'm on the edge of just giving up all the time.

I know what it's like to live on the edge now.

As you may know I'm in the process of moving house, that is stressful enough in itself but trying to arrange for three children to start GCSE, A-level and college courses at the same time, sort out buses to school, uniforms & college equipment is insane.

Coupled with the fact that we have other 'things' going on in life which I'm not able to talk about at the moment makes for a very stressful time.

I can feel that permanent burden almost physically resting on my head, the pressure is behind my eyes and manifests as a permanent headache.

Yes, I know what it's like to live on the edge.

The toughest thing is doing all this alone, not alone in the sense that there is no one around me, but alone in the sense that I'm not complete without Claire. We faced these trials in life together, it was always 'Mark and Claire' – that was how we lived. My coping habits and strategies involve Claire and have been very well rehearsed over the last 22 years together and it takes more than three months to break these habits and install new strategies.

I feel like an amputee, like there's a part of my body missing. I feel like I'm the world's most accomplished drummer and I've just had my arm amputated.

==oh my god, I've just remembered Rick Allen from Def Leppard==

So after some YouTube-ing I've just found this video and I'm crying at it...

[https://youtu.be/shh2rXs0wLg or search "Def Leppard The One hand drummer doing a solo" on Youtube]

I remember seeing a TV show years ago about Rick when he lost his arm, he didn't know how he would ever complete his passion and play drums again, how could he, he only had one arm and who has ever heard of a one armed drummer?

But he decided that he'd do it, he redesigned the drum kit... Now I am no drummer, but from what I understand he redesigned it to use the upstroke of his knees which had never been done before. The result of that tweak to the drum kit was that he was now able to play things that no other drummer could... All with one arm.

The video above is only 30 seconds long, but I have now watched it six times.

It inspires me, it motivates me and I'm now really glad I wrote this blog post, because I was on the edge of not bothering.

Tagged

· On the Edge

56. Month 5 Week 22 Day 148 Her absense is absent

Its been a while since I posted. Life has taken over and we've moved temporarily to my lovely sister's house in Devon whilst we wait for our house sale to exchange/complete, the kids are being settled in to their new school/college and I've moved my office down to my sister's study so that I can at least work. Life has taken over.

I've not had time to think about Claire recently. Her birthday was on the 5th September which just came and went – another first I guess, but one that just slipped past without so much as a sidewards glance – I guess life just took over.

With the house move creating so much uncertainty and the practicalities of trying to organise so many things and juggle so many balls I've not had time to think. In some ways that's a good thing.

The irony in this post is that life has taken over – life has taken over on a blog that is about the death of my wife.

I'm really looking forward to getting into our new house and beginning a new life. I want to include Claire in my life again as at the moment she seems so absent, no photographs on the wall, no familiar surroundings and none of those old routines.

All of this allows me to realise that whilst grieving is a painful thing to do it's actually extremely healing, it's progress, it's moving forwards and it's good to do. Because life is on hold at the moment I've had to put grieving on hold, and I miss it.

In an abstract way, her absence is absent and that feels really odd!

Tagged

- Absence

57. Month 5 Week 23 Day 154 I miss you, Claire, I miss you, I miss you, I miss you

I miss you Claire, I miss you, I miss you.
   I miss holding you.
   I miss seeing you.
   I miss kissing you.
   I miss the warmth of you next to me in bed at night.
   I miss your kindness.
   I miss your love.
   I miss the feel of your skin.
   I miss seeing you first thing in the morning and last thing at night.
   I miss telling you about the day.
   I miss hearing about your day.
   I miss your guidance.
   I miss your approval.
   I miss your presence.
   I miss hearing your voice.
   I miss joking with you.
   I miss you taking the mickey out of me.
   I miss your laughing.
   I miss your crying.
   I miss your comfort.
   I miss comforting you.
   I miss you Claire, I miss you, I miss you.

Tagged

- Missing her

58. Month 6 Week 25 Day 171 Absolute Clarity

Well, I finally have an Internet connection in my own house and can now get back to posting. Since I last wrote an update we have moved 150 miles away to the beautiful Dorset coast – something Claire always wanted to do.

It's been a mixed bag of emotions from absolute delight that we are living in such a gorgeous house in perfect surroundings to absolute dismay that Claire isn't here to share it.

We are living the dream but unfortunately it was Claire's dream too – I'm not sad for myself I'm just sad that Claire never got to see it. She was so close, she knew she would be moving, she chose this house with me and we decided to move here together... But she didn't quite make it.

It just brings back the importance to me of living in the moment.

I have a wonderful coach and friend coming to stay with me for two days towards the end of October to unravel the tangled thoughts in my mind. I know it will be painful but I know it will be healing too. As part of that process I know she will ask me to set a goal for my new life, so I've been thinking, what should be in that goal what do I want to achieve?

Fast cars, fast living, lots of holidays, financially independent living and big houses are the first things which come into mind. But losing Claire has changed me fundamentally, as it will have changed everyone that knew her.

My goal now consists of working towards living each day with exquisite joy, living each moment so consciously that I can enjoy just being alive. It might sound silly but it occurs to me that we live life focusing so much on the things around us and planning for the future which might never happen. And this comes at the expense of enjoying the now.

It's all still slightly tangled in my head, which I know is going to be Emma's job to sort out at the end of October (good luck gal!), so it doesn't make complete sense yet but it will, and I'm looking forward to when it reaches absolute clarity.

Tagged

- change
- clarity
- goals

59. Month 6 Week 26 Day 181 Wine Glasses, George Benson and Tears

I've been a bit up and down this weekend. I need some new wine glasses as most of ours had smashed so when I was in Morrisons I picked up a new set, you know those enormous ones that can fit half a bottle in each glass. We've got a set like that in the caravan that the two of us used to share when we went away on little trips, and drinking a glass of wine on Saturday night from my new mega-wineglass reminded me so much of what I was missing with Claire.

A simple wineglass moved me to tears.

Then on Sunday night I fancied listening to some music whilst I cooked dinner, as I was browsing through the records I came across George Benson so on he went. Within a few minutes the music was cranked up loud and I was singing and dancing to "Love Times Love", and then I caught myself. I caught myself singing and dancing and remembering that George Benson was the first CD I ever bought twentysomething years ago just after we got married... And again I was in tears.

I think it's the sharing of memories that is so difficult. We all have memories of things we've done in the past and normally I would have just said to Claire "Hey, these wine glasses remind me of the ones we've got in a caravan" or "wow, do you remember dancing around our tiny living room in our first house to this track 20 years ago" and the conversation would have been over. But it would have been a conversation, and now I have those things to say but there's no one there to say them to, it's almost like they are pointless memories!

I get these 'moments' quite often. Moments of memories that are triggered by the most mundane things. Moment of complete sadness, complete loneliness and complete desperation. I so desperately want to have a conversation with her. Just to share those memories again... We were together for nearly 30 years so there are quite a lot of memories!

What I am very clear about however is that I'm not going to punish myself over it, I know she's not coming back, I know that I have to find a way of coping with those memories (which are all good by the way).

So here's what I'm going to do.

At Claire's funeral we had some memory cards printed and asked people to write down their fondest memory of Claire, I have them all treasured in a box in my wardrobe and from now on I'm going to add my own memories.

Each time I have a 'moment' triggered by a memory I'll write it down and add it to the collection and watch the collection of happy memories grow...

Tagged

- coping
- memories

60. Month 6 Week 27 Day 184 It's been 6 months

It's six months today since my beautiful Claire left us, so I have decided to read back through this blog at some of the old posts. When I set this website up I did it because I wanted to keep a record of how far I'd come, I knew it would be easy to spend my whole life wallowing so six months seems like a good time to reflect a little on how things are going.

The pain

On 21 April I wrote a post and it simply said " I slept last night and got some respite from the pain" – I remember that pain, it was that sharp excruciating kind of pain that comes from a deep cut or broken bone. It was the kind of pain that I can imagine people banging their head against a wall to stop. That raw pain has stopped, it's now a dull ache, the kind of ache that we get in our knees or back as we get older. The kind of continuous pain that we get used to living with, but is actually liveable with.

Days of firsts

On 29th of April I talked about a day of firsts. There are still many more 'firsts' to come which I know may be challenging. Christmas is the obvious big one but what I have realised is that the things we miss so much are the old habits, the way we used to do things, the things we used to say or the routines that we had got into. And what I know for sure is that Claire is not those routines – she is far more than that.

Knowing that means that I can remove the meaning to those routines and begin to look for new routines and habits to create a new vision of things like Christmas.

Moving house as been a big help in this, it has forced us to create some new routines and habits in a completely different environment. It has allowed us to separate the things around us from the memory of Claire and find a way to bring her memory into a new environment with our new routines and habits.

Feeling connected again

In May I wrote about feeling disconnected, I commented that it felt as though I have had something amputated. Oddly that feeling has completely gone now and I feel very much connected to my Claire. I still miss her terribly and sometimes the slightest thing sets me off.. When I have one of those moments it can feel like I haven't come very far at all, but reading back to how I felt helps me to realise how much progress I've made.

Grief is a journey

I think what I have come to be aware of is that grief is an absolute journey. But it seems as though it's a journey without an end.

I've recently joined an excellent Private group on Facebook made up exclusively of men that have lost their wives recently. It has been enormously helpful in being able to share my thoughts with a group of people that truly understand. A common theme with grief though seems to be the need to return to 'normal'.

What I know for sure is that I need to let go of that terrible label 'normal'. It's simply a way of describing how things used to be and clearly they aren't like that any more, so the idea of 'normal' actually has no meaning at all.

My challenge for the next six months is to work on accepting our new 'normal'. Life is totally different now and it always will be which I guess is why grief is such a journey. As a family we need to continue to build our new habits and routines and find ways to include the memory of Claire so that this becomes our new, and perfectly acceptable 'normal'.

I feel like someone on a journey hacking a path through the jungle, with absolutely no idea where I'm going and even struggling at times to keep going. Yet I can also imagine that if I were to take a moment and just look back at where I had come from I would see it clearly worn path which is clear and ready for the kids to tread.

I've still no idea where I'm going, but I'm going to keep on hacking as at least I'm making progress!

Tagged

- Grieving

61. Month 7 Week 29 Day 199 What does it mean?

It's so easy to attribute meaning to things isn't it? The things we wear, the things we say and the things we do mean different things to different people and it's often hard to separate out the truth from the fiction. Does it REALLY mean that?

I read an excellent blog post recently [1] by another widower named Michael Adams where he talks about the meaning behind whether guys in our situation should wear a wedding ring or not. You see a wedding ring means I am married, and yet as Michael explains the truth is I'm not. However for me I feel like I still am and so I continue to wear my wedding ring. Wearing a ring means one thing to one person and another to someone else.

Another one of these 'means' problems has being moving through the grieving process. On the one hand I know it's good to begin to rebuild my life but on the other hand it means I'm moving further away from Claire and the life that we had. But does it really mean that? Is it possible to rebuild and draw closer to her? Does rebuilding genuinely mean moving further away?

It's so easy to link the two halves of a 'means' statement and act out as if X truly does mean Y, when in reality it is just a sentence we have used to describe something and there is no real relationship between X and Y.

Of course I can rebuild my life and it is in no way connected with how close I feel to Claire.

Of course, whether I choose to wear my wedding ring or not is in no way connected with moving further away from Claire.

I may wear my wedding ring forever, or I may not. I'm at the stage

now where I can choose to do what I want and be happy with it –
and that 'means' whatever I want it to mean – or perhaps it means
nothing at all!

[1] http://www.clearlypositive.co.uk/widowers-wedding-ring/

Tagged

- Grieving
- Rings

62. Month 7 Week 30 Day 210 Love is

This post has the possibility to be cataclysmically misinterpreted, but I'm going to write it anyway because I want to document how I feel and I know others feel the same way when they have lost partners.

Words can't express how lonely I feel at the moment, and that is very definitely 'lonely' and not 'alone'. Those two words seem to have the same meaning on the face of it but they are so completely different, I'm surrounded by wonderful kids, supportive family and amazing friends who are doing everything they can (for which I am truly and eternally grateful) but it doesn't matter what anyone does there is no substitute for the love that is shared between partners.

There is something about the love of a partner that is so very different from anyone else. There are conditions to the love from a partner, it's not handed out because they are family or because they feel sorry for someone, the love from family and friends is unconditional, it's kind of compulsory because of the relationship. But the love of a partner is conditional, conditional upon that love being reciprocated and it feels very different to all the other kinds of love.

The love of a partner has to be worked at, it has to be noticed every day and it is completely two-way, and because it has to be worked at you feel it every time the other person extends their love towards you – and right now that love is missing. Not only missing from being given to me but missing in that I can't hand it out, and that feels cold... so very cold.

There's nothing that can replace noticing how beautiful Claire was, stroking her hair, giving her a peck on the cheek and then getting on with what ever I was doing. Even hearing the jingling of another woman's jewellery brings those emotions flooding back, or seeing someone wearing some clothes similar to what Claire wore reminds me that I can't just tell her I love her and give her that peck on the cheek – giving love and feeling love!

I posted this on Facebook last night, and I really mean it...

"If you have a partner, please go and hug them right now and notice how wonderful it feels to be so close to the one you love. I'm wishing I could do the same."

Tagged

- loneliness
- love
- what is love

63. Month 7 Week 31 Day 212 Do nothing, it helps

I'm reading an amazing book at the moment called 'Do Nothing', it's not specific to grief and loss but is specific to life in general... So I guess it pretty much applies to me as I think I'm still alive!

The themes within the book are familiar to me as I spent the last two years on bit of a personal development drive and what I'm discovering in this book is helping more, let me explain.

Since losing Claire I have been very aware of the label 'grief'. As soon as we choose to adopt a label like this then we can begin to act out everything we believe about that label, and so it becomes a self fulfilling prophecy. Many people believe they are 'an angry person' or perhaps they believe they are 'not coping' – these are just labels and so guess what happens... Yep, they begin to believe those labels and act them out which serves to reinforce the belief in the first place – a never ending cycle of destruction.

What we really need to understand is that we have an inside world and an outside world. The outside world is everything that goes on out there, everything that happens outside of our own mind, which is pretty much everything. We then have an inside world where we think about things and decide what the outside world means. We notice things but the problem is we delete more things than we notice and so our inside world becomes distorted.

The biggest problem is that the inside world IS the world to us, it is all that we know and it taints our view of everything outside of us.

We do indeed create our own world inside our own mind through the power of our own thought... comforting stuff if you really think about it.

And the solution to all this?

Understand that this is the process that we go through every time we experience something in the outside world (perhaps like losing a wife), in order to make sense of it we have to filter it through our own thought patterns and our own ideas of what is wrong and what is right. Once we understand this thought process we can change it, and we can change it to do nothing.

When we truly do nothing we apply none of our own warped filters. It leaves us clean, it leaves us true and it leaves us at peace.

I can honestly say that with the power of doing nothing I am at peace.

Ref: https://www.amazon.co.uk/Do-Nothing-Looking-Start-Living/dp/0957214502 .

Tagged

- do nothing
- peace

64. Month 8 Week 32 Day 223 1st Holiday Season Without A Loved One – HUFFPOST LIVE

Late on Friday afternoon I was contacted by the Huffington Post live broadcasting to see if I would be willing to participate in their HuffPost Live shows which will look at the topic of coping with the loss of a loved one over Christmas, I admit I was a little nervous because I didn't really know what was going to happen but you know me, I just went for it and said okay.

Without any prompting from me the grief counsellor Dr Judith Johnson mentioned my favourite phrase "live in the now", well how nice it was to hear someone else say that this is what we should do. She took it a little further and said that it would be good to not have too many plans for Christmas, who knows how we are going to feel at any given point, and if we have made definite plans and don't feel up to it on the day then it can be rather stressful if we are unable to say no.

So in the run-up to Christmas if I have agreed to be somewhere or to do something and I let you down at the last minute, forgive me. And likewise, if you have agreed to be somewhere or do something with me and you let me down at the last minute, don't worry about it.

My plan for Christmas is to have no plan and right now that's just the way I like it.

Tagged

- Christmas

65. Month 8 Week 32 Day 224 Our natural healing process

I had a bit of a revelation yesterday whilst thinking about what I would talk about on the Huffington Post live interview. It's strange how these revelations can happen at the weirdest of times and I was driving the car when this one hit me.

I was thinking about healing, and it occurred to me that if we cut ourselves or injure ourselves physically we don't instantly start running to the doctors to ask how we are going to heal. We don't get worried about where we are in the process of healing, should blood have clotted by now? What should my haemoglobin level be for this cut to heal? When exactly will the two ends of this broken bone begin to knit back together, what is the process and how long will each stage of that process take? We don't bother with any of that, we just trust our bodies innate ability to heal these wounds at the right pace and at the right time.

So why do we think it should be any different with emotional injuries?

Could it be that if I just don't bother wondering what stage of the grieving process I'm at or how long it's going to take that my mind will just heal itself?

The more I think about that, or rather, the more I don't think about healing the more peaceful it becomes. I can see there is no need to worry or be concerned about anything, I trust my mind and body to do what it needs to do, when it needs to do it.

I think that sometimes the temptation is to try to rationalise things and get our highly educated brains working on solving the problem of how do we overcome our grief. But the reality is when we do this we ironically get in the way of the healing process and our highly educated brains interfere with the natural healing process, much like we tell a child not to pick their scab on a recently grazed knee. "It'll never get well if you pick it" I can hear my mother telling me now...

So I'm not going to pick this scab, I'll let my mind do what it needs to do when it needs to do it, and that's just fine.

Tagged

· Healing
· Natural
· Process

66. Month 8 Week 33 Day 230 Not looking forward to Christmas

This is one of those post where I have no idea where it's going but I have to get this off my chest.

I'm not looking forward to Christmas one bit.

Christmas in our house was always organised by Claire. She did all of the present thinking and the buying, she sorted out the kids' stockings and wrote all the Christmas cards. On one level these are all practical things which I'm okay at, kind of like getting the house work done, the dog walked or the washing sorted – bung it in a spreadsheet, print it and put it on the kitchen wall and it happens. But Christmas is more than just the practical buying presents and writing cards, it needs some thought.

Presents need to be carefully selected for the right individual and the right words need to be written into a Christmas card for it to mean anything, or what is the point?

I don't know what to write. It doesn't seem appropriate to wish all of the seasons happy blessings on someone else when I feel so desperately alone. I'm not filled with the joys of Christmas, I'm not bounding around the shops wanting to join in the festive fun, I'm just sitting here alone wanting my Claire back!

What do I want for Christmas? Guess!

This is a time of year for families to get together, and that's one thing I AM looking forward to – we've got almost everyone coming to ours this year which will be tough, but good to be all together.

The problem with this time of year is the constant reminders that she's not here that is so difficult to bear.

- My wife hasn't asked me what I want for Christmas this year.
- I've got no-one to surprise with an oddball gift that only she knows what it means.
- So many cards that have WIFE written on them, and as with everything, when something is on your mind that's all you see.

I suppose it depends on how we look at those reminders. (This feels like clutching at straws for me right now but I'm desperately holding onto any positive thought that I have). Each time I'm reminded she's not here and it hurts it's also a reminder that she was so lovely, so loving and kind and that I am one lucky guy to have experienced that.

I've now reminded myself of this that I read out at her funeral... now may be a good time to revisit it!

> You can close your eyes and pray that she'll come back or you can open your eyes and see all she's left.
> Your heart can be empty because you can't see her or you can be full of the love you shared.
> You can turn your back on tomorrow and live yesterday or you can be happy for tomorrow because of yesterday.
> You can remember her and only that she's gone or you can cherish her memory and let it live on.
> You can cry and close your mind, be empty and turn your back or you can do what she'd want: smile, open your eyes, love and go on.

Tagged

- Christmas

67. Month 8 Week 33 Day 232 Please continue sharing

I've just had another one of those moments when I've realised something and I want to get it down in writing as soon as possible.

Because of this website I've been in contact with so many other people that have lost their partners that I decided to set up a secret Facebook group for us all to chat. We currently have 15 'members' and we share our stories and thoughts with each other and I want to share with you a brief story from the group.

People often say to me that my story is shocking, we lost Claire so rapidly, she was seemingly fighting fit in the morning and gone by the evening – no history of any illness, no signs and no symptoms until her body started to shut down. We had no time to say goodbye, in fact we didn't know that we needed to because we just thought she had a stomach bug.

A good friend of mine shared their story this morning and mentioned that their partner had cancer and went from 14 stone down to 5 stone. When I read that post I actually spoke out loud to myself in shock. I was just stunned that someone could lose so much weight.

Now here's the rub, if anyone loses someone prematurely it's always shocking, we all have that shocking story because dying young is just not the natural course of things. Our tendency in today's society is not to talk about death, and I admit to completely ignoring the subject myself up until 17th of April this year. But if we do talk about our feelings and share our stories we can quickly realise that we are not alone. In the darkness of our own thoughts and in the pain of our own stories it can feel like a terribly lonely place, and when we share we can realise that the world is full of beautiful and lovely people who genuinely do understand what we're feeling.

So I would encourage you to share your own story. Don't be afraid to tell others about how you really feel, I bet you'll discover they have a shocking story to tell too and suddenly neither of you are alone any more.

To the people that are sharing their stories with me, thank you, thank you, thank you.

Tagged

- updates

68. Month 8 Week 34 Day 238 My Last Christmas Card

Claire, I wanted to write my last ever Christmas card to you. At the time I wrote the one last year I never knew it would be the last one I would ever be able to give you, that leaves things a little unfinished... and so here's my final Christmas card I'll ever write to you:

"Dearest Claire,

Well, it's been quite a year again. So much has happened, we've moved house, the kids have changed schools and for whatever reason you have been taken from us. I never thought in a million years that 2013 would end like this.

But thank you for loving me this year, thank you for being there and thank you for being you.

I still love you more than you will ever know, and now you're gone I miss you so, so, so much.

You are still my angel, my saviour, my rock, my life and my everything – even though I've been writing that since we were 16!

I love you more than words or this poxy computer and website can ever explain.

Sleep tight my sweetheart, you can rest now.

M

xxxxxxx"

Tagged

- Coping
- Christmas

69. Month 8 Week 35 Day 240 Meltdown

Last night I admit to having bit of a meltdown. I've been chatting with a great guy on Facebook that has also recently lost his wife and he posted a comment about the number of years that they had been together, and he started counting those years from the moment they first kissed.

What a great way to answer the question "How long have you been together?" – it's not measured by years of marriage but by the years that a couple's hearts have been entwined, and that entwining begins when they first kiss.

I can remember that moment so clearly, we were at a Christmas disco, everyone knew we fancied each other (now there is a term that you can only use if you're 16! – Who says 'fancied' any more?) and there was a little too much cider flowing – someone was walking around with a big bunch of mistletoe and they held it over me and Claire... I don't think we needed much encouragement! That was the moment, that was the moment that our hearts entwined and we never let go.

But when was that moment?

I knew it was around Christmas but I couldn't remember exactly when, and then I remembered seeing the date written in Claire's little diary, but where was that diary?

And so the meltdown last night commenced. Hunting high and low, searching through old paperwork, files in my office and boxes which are still unpacked from when we moved.

As you can see I found that diary in the end hidden in a drawer in the bedside table underneath Claire's pyjamas which are still there. And there in Claire's own handwriting is the reminder of that date.

She had an uncanny ability to remember dates like that, she wouldn't have had to look for a diary to know... But I'm so glad she took the time to note it down, that day our hearts entwined is there in black and white and now it's etched into my mind too – 7th December 1985.

Thank you Claire for writing it down, I think a little part of you knew that someday I would need that diary and your note... and that day was yesterday, 28 years and 4 days after you wrote it. xxxxxx

Tagged

- Christmas
- First Kiss

70. Month 8 Week 35 Day 244 Grieving the old me

I have just seen this on a forum, it is extremely insightful and as I think about it now, it applies to me completely:

> "Loss definitely changes you as a person and I found myself not only grieving for <name removed>, but also grieving the old me"

I can feel this happening with myself. I know that I have changed fundamentally since losing Claire, I also think that it is inevitable that anyone that was close to her, with Claire playing a large part in their lives will also have changed inextricably. We've lost Claire and we've lost a lot of old selves.

This seems to be a double grief, a double loss – a loss of someone very special and a loss of our old 'self' which was in part governed by the person we have lost.

One can argue that we are not defined by the people who are around us and that we are our own selves, but for me I gave myself entirely to Claire. When we said our wedding vows I promised that I would give myself to her without question, and that is what I did. So she did define me, she was part of my character which is why I think we had such a great relationship... we acted as one, we were one character which clearly would lead to grieving for the "old me" also.

It would be easy to become extremely melancholy about that.

I happened to quite like the old me, I was comfortable with that person, so what now?

I guess it's a slow process of discovering a new me, and indeed it's the process for everyone that is experiencing that same thing to discover their new 'self'.

As I said we could become melancholy, but how about we view it as an opportunity? An opportunity to discover something new. An opportunity to discover a world which existed outside of our old 'self'. And in that respect, with that view of things, it goes from the melancholy to the exciting...

Tagged

- If
- Old Self
- New self

71. Month 9 Week 36 Day 252 Happy because of those Christmases past

Christmas is beginning to get a lot of people in my situation down. I take part in quite a few forums and discussion groups, they often help to share what's on my mind and know that I'm not going crazy or indeed that I'm not alone. These groups have lit up in the run-up to Christmas... It doesn't take much to understand why.

And yet, even though I too am not relishing the idea of spending my first Christmas without Claire, if I think about her I still feel warm and loved.

At Claire's funeral I read out a short poem, it's been repeated on this blog twice already so I'm not going to reproduce it here again in its entirety, but one line really stands out to me...

You can turn your back on tomorrow and live yesterday or you can be happy for tomorrow because of yesterday.

The love that Claire and I shared was truly special. I knew it was at the time but I can feel it even stronger now in a paradoxical kind of way. Tomorrow will be Christmas day. I can either turn my back on that day and live for all of the Christmases that have passed or I can be happy for Christmas Day because of all of those Christmases passed.

As I'm sitting here again struggling to hold it together, I feel so blessed that I had such a wonderful wife for so long.

Christmas Day might be difficult, Christmas Day might be easy. I'm not going to make a decision now and then let the day turn into a self fulfilling prophecy. The day will be what it is and I will rest, happy because of all those yesterdays.

Tagged

- Christmas

72. Month 9 Week 38 Day 264 That bitter/ sweet contrast

I caught up with an old friend yesterday that I haven't seen for 20 years, we had a lovely home cooked meal together and talked constantly for 9 hours straight. It was so nice to have a 1-2-1 chat with an adult that shares my view on life and understands to some degree what I am going through. Last night I felt human again for the first time in many many months.

And yet this morning I took the dog for a walk to the beach, it was a stormy morning (which I love by the sea) with the waves crashing against the shore line, and I felt so desperately lonely again – worse than before.

It's as though when I taste the sweetness of happiness the bitterness of loneliness tastes 10 times worse.

It's that sharp contrast from one state to the next that exacerbates the negative emotions of the negative state, I can certainly see the temptation in withdrawing from any activity that could be positive... it just makes coming back down to earth so much worse!

In the case of last night, I spent 9 hours in good company enjoying catching up with the past 20 years – of course we talked a lot about Claire but it was all positive and happy memories. Yet, not 1 hour after I got home, I was in bed in the dark and feeling totally lonely again.

A bi-polar existence is not one I ever imagined having.

With any of my blog posts I make an attempt to learn something new, to take something away from what I have written that I didn't know before, in that way I can grow and develop and continue discovering the new me... So what can be learned from this?

These emotions are normal and I'm not a freak.

I need to incorporate those bipolar experiences into one experience of life. Even as I'm writing I can see that I have compartmentalised the wonderful nine hours I spent yesterday and put them into a 'happy' box, which I am then comparing to being back home again which is in the 'lonely' box.

Of course these two boxes look different, they are at different ends of the spectrum... So I wonder what would happen if they were in the same box! If I didn't compartmentalise things and give them labels of 'happy' or 'lonely', and I just accepted them all as an experience of life then they would all be together in one big 'life' box and suddenly the bitter/sweet contrast is gone... And that feels so much better... and there I have the learning for today!

No need to write any more!

Tagged

- Contrast
- Happy

73. Month 9 Week 38 Day 265 A change of perspective

When I feel low I write. Writing helps me make sense of everything, it helps me put things in order.

Perspective 1

It's the loneliness that is truly getting to me at the moment, I'm not talking about being alone, I'm talking about being lonely. When I married Claire I meant every single word of our vows, I completely and utterly gave myself to her and I know she did to me also. From that moment, when the Rev David Pytches joined our hands together and raised them high, two people became one. And that was how we lived.

Claire has been gone eight months and I still talk about 'we'. "WE moved to Dorset because…", "WE bought this house because…" – it is just ingrained into my every thought and my every action that we do this together.

The result of living like this for 22 years is that I still want to share everything with her. When I see the waves crashing against the shoreline in the middle of the storm it only seems to have significance because I could talk about it with Claire. When I taste a glorious bottle of the finest red wine, it tastes so good because I could share that experience with Claire. Without sharing there seems to be no significance.

What's the point of seeing a beautiful sunset if there's no one to share it with?

What's the point of enjoying a lovely meal if there's no one to share it with?

Sharing is me, sharing digs to the root of who I am and without the ability to do that it seems to rock my identity. I don't know who I am any more.

I can't see any immediate resolution to it.

I guess time will find a way.

Perspective 2

This part is written with the exact same loneliness emotion in mind but I want to tackle it from a different perspective. I met with a wonderful friend the other day, our situations are different but we share similar experiences of loss, she wrote to me today:

> "I've developed a stronger and deeper relationship with [family and friends] that I wouldn't have had... and that has enriched my life enormously"

This statement made me stop in my tracks. Of course the pain of losing Claire cuts deep but sometimes those surgical cuts can also have a healing effect. I can definitely feel a deeper relationship with some family members since losing Claire, especially my wonderful kids. I can feel a deeper connection (rather intangible) but also notice things that are said and done (much more tangible) which never would have been said or done before.

In that sense, and with that frame of reference on the same situation, I can also see that my life has been enriched enormously.

Thank you O,T,T & M.... I love you guys.

Tagged

- Coping
- Loneliness

74. Month 9 Week 38 Day 266 I can't...

When I first thought about it I thought "I can't..."
   But I'm now at a place where I think "I can..."
   "I can begin to consider the possibility and imagine the options of what it would bring when I can" – and that is a far better place to be.

Tagged

- Coping
- Missing her
- Moving on

75. Month 9 Week 39 Day 267 A Claire and Bright Perspective

I saw this on Facebook yesterday, it was shared by a couple of friends that I have made who have also recently lost their partners. It really is quite moving.

"Grief can destroy you –or focus you. You can decide a relationship was all for nothing if it had to end in death, and you alone. OR you can realize that every moment of it had more meaning than you dared to recognize at the time, so much meaning it scared you, so you just lived, just took for granted the love and laughter of each day, and didn't allow yourself to consider the sacredness of it.

But when it's over and you're alone, you begin to see that it wasn't just a movie and a dinner together, not just watching sunsets together, not just scrubbing a floor or washing dishes together or worrying over a high electric bill. It was everything, it was the why of life, every event and precious moment of it. The answer to the mystery of existence is the love you shared sometimes so imperfectly, and when the loss wakes you to the deeper beauty of it, to the sanctity of it, you can't get off your knees for a long time, you're driven to your knees not by the weight of the loss but by gratitude for what preceded the loss. And the ache is always there, but one day not the emptiness, because to nurture the emptiness, to take solace in it, is to disrespect the gift of life."— Dean Koontz, Odd Hours

When I read this section "... you're driven to your knees not by the weight of the loss but by gratitude for what preceded the loss" it reduced me to tears. I'm not ashamed to admit that I have not had a good time for a couple of days, I've felt confused, lost and bewildered. But things are settling now a little and clarity is starting to appear.

I re-read some of my old blog posts last night and one of them stood out, a post where I was talking about my reason for living. Looking to the future can seem so bleak with the loneliness and loss being so huge and sometimes it seems like a struggle to keep going, what reason do I have?

And then the reason becomes clear, the reason is Claire. (Oh yes, the fact that the Latin meaning of the name Claire is 'clear and bright' is not lost on me).

I truly am reduced to my knees, not only because of the loss of Claire but by the gratitude for the 28 years we shared together. When I think about all of those years it makes me want to shout in gratitude, to dance around like an idiot, to scream from the top of my lungs about how good our relationship was.

It's those emotions that make things so tough and yet conversely give me a reason to go on.

Those emotions are the life taker and the life giver at the same time, all I have to do is choose which one they are going to be – it's all a matter of perspective.

Tagged

· Reasons

76. Month 9 Week 39 Day 269 Keep facing the same way

I think it's quite natural to grieve for the past and all that we had when we have lost someone so close. We think about the happy memories, the times we enjoyed together, the impact we had on each other's lives and the fact that all of that is gone. For the past nine months the past is the direction I have been facing, all of my emotions have been focused on what I've lost.

The revelation I had last night was that I've turned a corner, I'm still painfully aware of the past but I'm now looking to the future.

The problem is that the future seems quite grim at the moment. It seems dark, cold, lonely and empty.

I've been struggling with these emotions over the past few days and now I can see why, I have dared for the first time to consider my future.

And whilst I feel at the depth of my loneliness when I look to the future I know that this is actually a good thing. I know that I have turned a corner, I have begun to consider my future which is a positive step. Dwelling and wallowing in the past won't allow me to move onwards, although right at the moment that first step onwards seems rather unattractive.

Dwelling on the past has served me well up until this point, I guess I have become used to it. Looking to the future is a far more painful experience right at the moment, but I know that deep within me things will be okay. I know that looking to the future is the right thing to do and I know that, in time, the heavy weight of loneliness, which seems to stretch in front of me, will lift also.

Sometimes it's simpler to take the easy option, it's simpler to remain focused on the past... Even though it's painful to think of what I've lost it's easier than thinking about the future.

Beginning to consider my future is the most painful thing I've experienced since actually losing Claire. The temptation to remain in the past is immense, it's painful there but familiar, so it's safe. All I need to do is keep going, keep facing the same way and accept that the pain of uncertainty about the future will allow me to experience the emotions even more when it lifts.

Tagged

· Feeling

77. Month 9 Week 39 Day 270 Why is the pain of losing a partner so great?

The pain of losing a Claire seems so massive at the moment, I'm hoping that listing the reasons why would help me to understand them better and perhaps help others to also.

Losing a life partner is like losing part of yourself.

When we got married I gave myself so entirely and completely to Claire, I gave up my right to being an individual, two people became one. Without her here it feels as though one of my major organs is not functioning properly and that I am chronically ill in some way.

Making decisions.

When you lose a life partner you lose part of your decision-making process. We made decisions together, even if it wasn't an explicit joint decision it was always a joint decision nonetheless. If I wanted something to happen I would hint about it to Claire, she would then let me know if she agreed... And so the joint decision was made. Nothing explicit, everything implied, we just knew.

Off loading.

At the end of the day we used to tell each other what had happened, the good, the bad and the ugly. It was a coping strategy, after all, a problem shared is a problem halved! It was the way that we finished the day, the day always finished by sharing what had happened, enjoying the good things and resolving the bad things. Without her here that resolution is harder to reach.

Enjoying the good things.

When you have a life partner part of your strategy for enjoying things is to share with that person. If you see a beautiful sunset or taste a glorious bottle of red wine it always seems that much better when you share it with the person you have given your life to, so when that person is taken away from you your ability to enjoy those things declines.

Referencing.

Many people are either internally referenced or externally referenced. This means that they either intrinsically know that a decision they have made is a good one, or they need external verification from other people. Highly successful business people are often internally referenced, they just know they are brilliant and don't need anyone to tell them.

Well I was 'Claire' referenced. Yes, I know strictly speaking that is being externally referenced, but it is linked to a specific person. If I was a little unsure about what I was doing, whether it be in business or life I would ask Claire. She would be my barometer, and if the barometer pointed in a negative direction it meant I had to stop and vice versa. Without her I have no idea if I'm doing the right thing.

For everything that we do in life we have a strategy, we have a strategy for making decisions, coping at the end of the day, enjoying things, resolving things plus thousands more. When you give yourself so totally to another person your strategies for life become intertwined, so when that person is taken away it leaves you almost unable to function.

When you live with someone for 22 years they become part of you, they become who you are and when they die it challenges you in absolutely every aspect of your life. I have been challenged over these past nine months and I continue to be so more than ever.

Tagged

· Strategy

78. Month 9 Week 39 Day 272 Where is there?

Since the New Year a few people have contacted me and asked me how I'm doing, my reply has been fairly standard – "I'm getting there".

But where is 'there'? Is 'there' a destination?

When I arrive there will I know, will I be able to say with all certainty that I have arrived where ever 'there' is and that everything is now better?

The reality is that this is not going to happen. Claire has gone and she is never coming back, the only resolution is if she was, the only way that I would get 'there' is if Claire came back... But she's not going to so 'there' as a destination doesn't exist.

'There' is the journey, it's a journey which had a beginning but only ends when I do.

'There' is now the journey of my life, it's the journey of all of our lives that knew Claire.

'There' isn't the destination, it's the process, the path, the experience.

'There' isn't about feeling better or feeling worse, it's simply about feeling.

'There' is all around us, it is us, it is life, this life – so yes... I'm getting 'there'.

Tagged

· Feeling

79. Month 9 Week 40 Day 275 Feeling Angry?

I feel compelled to write this post as a response to some of the messages I'm getting and seeing at the moment. Normally I write about my own emotions and how I am dealing with them, I guess in some ways this post isn't so different, but the reason for writing it is not to help myself, it's to help others that seem to be struggling.

Anger seems to be a big issue with many people in my situation. Angry at the situation itself, angry at the turn of events that unfolded when their loved one died and indeed angry at their late partner for leaving them so early in life.

I can honestly say I feel none of this anger. I feel completely calm and relaxed in this respect, not because of my own ability to deal with anything better then anybody else but because I believe I have an understanding of how our mind works. What I would like to do in this blog post is share how I look at the situation, the turn of events and the fact that Claire left me so early in her life.

A difference between what we think happens and what really happens.

The easiest way to describe this is to put it into a diagram.

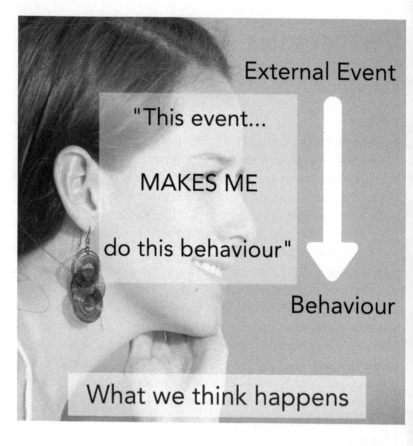

External Event

"This event...

MAKES ME

do this behaviour"

Behaviour

What we think happens

What we often think happens when we get angry (a behaviour) when something happens (external event) is that the external event MAKES us angry. Something happens, our blood begins to boil, our faces go red and we can feel the anger welling up inside. We seem to create a direct link between that external event and our own behaviour. The two seem inextricably linked... "That happened which makes me angry" – "they died and left me and that makes me angry" are common thoughts.

But this is not what really happens, this is taking the external event and behaviour and not accepting that we've done anything with that external event in our head. It's as though the event has led to a behaviour and we haven't been part of that process, but we have haven't we? We are completely part of it because we absorb that external event via our senses, we take everything we see, hear and feel about that external event, run it around inside our head which then leaves us with a behaviour.

So this is what really is happening.

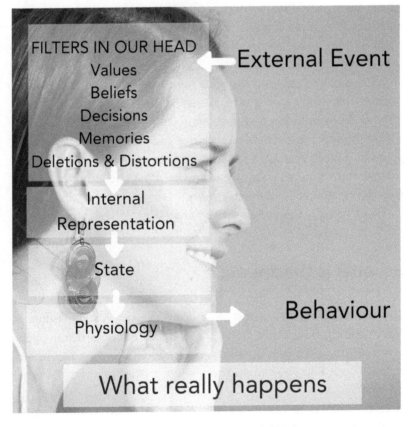

FILTERS IN OUR HEAD
Values
Beliefs
Decisions
Memories
Deletions & Distortions

Internal
Representation

State

Physiology

External Event

Behaviour

What really happens

What actually happens is that an external event enters our thought process via our senses. We then generalise things ("last time someone died then I felt this way") we delete things we can't make sense of, we have our own innate ways of doing things ("...this is just the way I handle life"), we have our own belief systems (you may believe that you deserve more, or that something is right or wrong... But who says?). You may have decided years ago that life wasn't fair, this could be a limiting decision which has led to limiting beliefs that your life is going to all go wrong, and when something negative happens it becomes a self-fulfilling prophecy ("yeh, I knew something shit would happen").

These are all filters inside your head, these filters completely change the reality of the external event. These filters give you an internal representation of that event in your head.

That internal representation changes your state, your blood boils, your heart races and you can feel the anger welling.

That state changes your physiology, your face becomes red, your fists clench and your stomach churns.

The physiology then affects your behaviour... You become angry.

So what is the answer?

This process happens in the blink of an eye but it's like a steam train heading down the wrong track. Once that steam train gets momentum and heads down the wrong track there's no stopping it, there's nothing you can do, there is just an inevitability about the situation.

So the trick is to put in a set of points early on in the process so that that steam train can choose an alternate heading. If we divert the train early enough in the process it won't regain the momentum and won't end up in the destination called anger.

I find myself in an awful situation, the external event that happened to me is that I lost my beautiful Claire.

I know that there are things that I would generalise about that situation, I will delete things that I can't make sense of, I have beliefs about the way my life should have turned out and I have a wonderful memories together. All of these act as filters in my mind and distort that original event. I know that I'm doing this. I know that I have created my own internal representation of that horrible external event.

Because I know that I have done this I can choose to put in a set of points and divert the steam train.

My reality of losing Claire is entirely constructed in my head and that is the only place that reality exists. And when you realise that, when you realise that your thoughts are just that... They are only thoughts. Your thoughts are not reality, reality happens outside of you and you make sense of it with thoughts.

Now you know this, now you know that the way you feel is because of your thoughts... Have that thought, recognise it as a thought, and let it go...

Tagged

· Anger

80. Month 9 Week 40 Day 276 What did Claire teach me?

When Claire was alive she gave herself wholly to me. She dedicated her life to looking after me, caring for me and taking care of me. I did the same for her.

I now have a choice, I can either forget all of that or I can take what I learnt from Claire and use it to help me as I go into my future, so what did I learn from her? What made Claire so special and what did she teach me? She taught me:

To love with no strings attached, no hidden agendas, no mind games just straight forward and honest love.

That when we give ourselves to others we receive far more in return.

That tomorrow may never come, if it's worth doing, do it today.

To resolve all disagreements or arguments and never let them stew – we can't control other people, but we can control our own response and we can forgive them even if they don't forgive us.

To keep going no matter what.

To be aware of ourselves and our impact on the way we think and the way we perceive others.

That scientific research is not the be all and end all, operator bias, confirmation bias, complexity and many other factors affect the validity of so-called 'scientific' proof. Sometimes we just 'know' what is true.

To trust your heart as well as your head.

That living by the sea really is a calming place to be.

To take time for myself.

To enjoy a decent bottle of wine.

All I can do now is bundle up that little box of learning, tie it with a neat bow (just as Claire would have done) tuck it under my arm and carry it with me for the rest of my life.

Thank you my dear, you continue to be an inspiration to me.

Tagged

· Learning

81. Month 10 Week 40 Day 279 This too shall pass

I feel very strongly that I have turned a corner, a corner of acceptance, not necessarily acceptance of losing Claire but acceptance of the emotions attached to that. I'm still often overwhelmed with the love that I feel for her and then I become overwhelmed with loneliness and loss. I go from high to low in the blink of an eye.

I can wake up one morning and feel good, or I can wake up one morning and feel terrible.

One minute I can be focused on the task in hand and the next my mind can be wondering in 100 different directions.

I've reached a point of acceptance of these dichotomous emotions. They are the way things are, and each of them shall pass.

When I'm feeling good it keeps me grounded to know that things can change quite quickly and I will probably feel low again.

When I'm feeling low it keeps me hopeful to know that things can change quite quickly and I will feel happy again.

Whatever happens, however I feel at any given moment... This too shall pass.

Tagged

- Acceptance
- Happy
- Feeling Low
- This too shall pass

82. Month 10 Week 41 Day 286 Comparing

Through the power of the Internet I have been in contact with some amazing people that have inspired me and motivated me to make big changes in my life. I recently met up with Robin, he lost his wife just a few days before Claire died, we met up a couple of weeks ago for a lovely walk in the country and had a great lunch together, we shared our experiences and a good friendship has developed.

Robin also writes a blog about losing his beloved wife Sarah and last week he wrote this one... It touched me enormously. [http://lifewithoutsarah.blogspot.co.uk/2014/01/24-jan-2014-photo-of-day.html]

It seems to me that our propensity to compare the past with now is something that we just do. But I wonder, if we stopped comparing how much more could we enjoy the now?

If we went out for dinner and a meal we eat is good, but not quite as good as the time we went before, it is only because we have been comparing it that we are not enjoying it so much. If we just look at the meal in isolation, the meal we are eating right now, then we can enjoy it for what it is.

Yes, that is such a simple analogy, but it works doesn't it?

Today is only a horrible day if we compare it with a previous day. If we don't compare with anything that's gone before we can truly enjoy where we are, where we are at, what we are doing and who we are with uniquely for the current experience of now.

And you know what, I actually don't want to compare today with yesterday. As long as I compare my life now to my life with Claire it could always make today look grey. But the reality is that it is not.

Today is just today and it can be enjoyed for being today. I'm living in a wonderful part of the world now, I enjoy fresh sea air daily and am eating the healthiest food I've ever had. The years I had with Claire were fabulous and I loved every single moment and it's because I loved every single moment that I can enjoy today. Comparing today and indeed my future with my past isn't respecting the years I had with Claire at all.

So I'm not going to compare any more, in fact there is no comparison, how can there be? Today is unique. The life I am living now is completely different to the life I lived before. There is no comparison, on December 7th 1985 when Claire and I first kissed a chapter in my life opened and when she died on April 17th 2013 it closed. That chapter was beautiful and comparing anything to that isn't giving my life with Claire or the life I lead now the justice that either of them deserves.

With no comparing, today becomes wonderful, it's beautiful and it is valued for what it is, in it's own right without any comparison to what went before, we can then enjoy today and retain those wonderful memories of what went before.

Tagged

· Comparing

83. Month 10 Week 42 Day 292 A finite vessel or bottomless pit?

As I'm working through the issues that present themselves after losing Claire some things are beginning to strike me in quite a profound way. When something like this happens we seem to use phrases like "I'm at my wits end","I have nothing left", "it's all gone..." I know I have used these phrases myself several times and when I do I challenge myself to think about what I have said a little deeper and I think I've had it wrong for a while.

When we think in these ways it's as though we are looking at our body as a finite vessel with finite emotions and finite resources. We seem to view it as though we have only a certain amount of forgiveness, love, respect, strength etc to carry on, but what a limiting way of viewing our infinitely resourceful selves.

I'm constantly challenged to dig deeper and deeper yet constantly surprised to find more and more. It just keeps coming – my ability, indeed our ability, to love, forgive, respect (plus loads more) never ends. We're not a finite vessel we are a bottomless pit, we aren't born with resources that get used up, the truth is that they just keep on coming.

So if that's true why don't we dig deeper and deeper faster and faster? If all of these resources seem to replenish and keep on coming then let's use as much as we can.

It is so inspiring to notice our own internal strength to keep going, I remember when I first started jogging I could go at a slow pace for 2 min at a time before I required a one-minute walking breather. By practising every other day, and pushing myself a little harder each time I soon got this 2 min up to 30 min, and then 40 min and then an hour. My body just kept on responding in an amazing way, the more I pushed the more it gave. I didn't ask my body to do it it just responded, all I had to do was put in the effort and it just did it.

So as I'm finding that our mind responds in a similar way, and keeps on providing the resources we need in a never-ending pit of resourcefulness I'm going to keep digging, and the more I dig the stronger I get and the stronger I get the harder I can dig.

If digging is the order of the day, I'm off to exchange my little shovel for a great big JCB...

Tagged

- Strength

84. Month 10 Week 43 Day 300 Dealing with grief

I thought in this post I would share some of my own experiences of dealing with grief, and I mean dealing with grief, not living with it, not ignoring it, not pushing it to one side as if it doesn't exist, but actually dealing with it on a day-to-day basis, or even a minute-to-minute basis.

I guess it comes from spending two years developing myself that I know we all experience significant emotional events in our life at some point, these can have huge impacts on the way we view things in the future. We all know that we have beliefs about ourselves and some of those beliefs are **empowering** (I am good enough, I am strong) and some of those beliefs are **disempowering** (I don't deserve it, I'm not worth it). From the moment the consultant came into that little room and told me that Claire had died I knew this was a significant emotional event where one of those limiting and damaging beliefs could easily have been adopted.

"I don't deserve this", "why did it happen to me", "I'm worth more than this", "she's worth more than this", "she doesn't deserve it"... All would be easy thoughts to adopt yet all are **dis-empowering** decisions and beliefs.

I knew that from the moment I was told that I no longer had a wife any decision I made had to be empowering. I had to continue with life and I knew that from the second the consultant told me.

Not one single day, and I mean not one single day has passed without me working on myself. Every thought, every emotion, every single nagging idea that has dared to enter my brain has been dealt with. I'm working on the way I think 24 hours a day (and yes, I believe that my unconscious mind is also working on it whilst I am asleep).

The decision I made when Claire died was that I had to deal with it and I had to continue to live my life in a way that respected the 28 wonderful years I spent with Claire. Pushing those thoughts, emotions and nagging ideas to one side and not dealing with them has never been an option for me. I have faced them all head on and at the beginning they were hitting me literally every minute. Every minute of every day I was being pummelled with these thoughts, but because I have dealt with them as they have arrived things are much quieter now.

My program of self development with NLP and Hypnosis gave me a toolbox of techniques, ideas and thinking patterns that have allowed me to work on those thought processes – no longer do I fill up that great big dustbin of negativity that so many people carry around on their backs all day, getting heavier and heavier as the years go by – in fact I went into this whole process with a dustbin that had had a hand grenade chucked in it to completely clean it out, and as the days go by I refuse to fill that dustbin up again... it remains as clean today as it has ever been.

I genuinely feel at peace, those negative emotions and thoughts have almost stopped. Instead, they have been replaced by love. Love for everything that Claire was, everything that she did for me, everything that she did for the children and indeed immense love for her as my wife and best friend. I would much rather welcome those thoughts and emotions into my mind and allow them to live there rather than all of the negative ones.

If we are to make room for all of the positivity then we need to deal with the negativity. I continue to do so and will continue for the rest of my life.

Tagged

- Coping
- Decisions
- Hypnosis
- NLP

85. Month 10 Week 44 Day 303 Swimming

The journey I am on is a journey with a very distinct beginning, yet it is a journey without an end. Imagine walking down the beach towards the sea, taking the first tentative step as the waves break around your feet and walking out deeper and deeper into the ocean. As the water surrounds you you realise at some point you need to start swimming and so you just swim, further and further away from the shoreline.

The further you get from where you were the more lost you become until eventually the shoreline, and everything you know disappears completely from view. As you lose sight of where you were, you have no idea which direction to go in, and so you have only one option, keep swimming, keep swimming.

And whilst that analogy holds true we wouldn't really do that would we, we wouldn't just walk out into the sea and begin swimming? If we wanted to swim the English Channel we would have a support vessel, we'd cover our bodies in a protective layer to keep us warm, we would inform the Coastguard of where we were going, we would avoid all the large ships which crossed our path and eventually, with the aid of everything around us we would reach the other side.

And yet, even with all this help, I'm sure that when the sight of land disappears behind us and has yet to appear in front of us, it could seem as though we are in the middle of the channel with nothing but pain and torture in front of us. It's only the sheer determination to keep going that would keep us on our path to the other side.

The difference with grief is that there isn't another side, there isn't a destination. There is only the journey. And yet, with the support of those around us, our own internal resources and the sheer determination that we all possess. We can just keep swimming, swimming, swimming.

And as I keep on swimming it becomes easier to accept that this is my life now, it becomes easier to accept that I can no longer see the shoreline from where I started. It was a lovely shoreline, I spent many happy years relaxing on it and enjoying being there, but it's gone, it has disappeared from sight and will never return.

I've no idea which way to go on this journey, I'm just going to pick a direction and keep tenaciously swimming, accepting the help of those around me to act as my support vessel and just keep on going until the glorious day that grief turns in to love and I sight land ahead.

Tagged

- Coping
- Acceptance

86. Month 11 Week 46 Day 322 I WISH...

I wish...

Actually I don't. I refuse to go down the thought pattern of "I wish..." there are so many possibilities that I could wish for, I could wish Claire had never died, I could wish she'd been taken to the doctor earlier, I could wish she had fought harder to stay alive, I could wish I had come home early from work and gone to the hospital with her. All of those wishes are false hopes, all of those wishes will never come true and therefore all of those wishes are pointless and downright damaging, they lead to a world of blame and guilt which is totally unhealthy.

Living in the world of "I wish..." is a world surrounded by the past, it's a world where nothing moves on, it's a world that is locked in a place which is contrary to the truth and what actually happened.

"I wish..." is a very destructive thought pattern and I refuse to go there.

"I wish..." also damages the future. Living in the past by saying "I wish..." means we can feel guilty about enjoying life to come. It means feeling guilty about moving forwards in life, feeling happy, meeting a new partner, moving house and enjoying things again... And all because we are living in the past.

You can honor your past
You can treasure your past
You can and should love your past
You do not have to live in your past

So do I wish it had all never happened? Well, to be honest, I refuse to answer that question. I refuse to be drawn into the world of negativity wishing things hadn't happened when actually they did. My answer? Deal with what has happened and stop wishing for something else to happen that is an impossibility... That is a world of misery, despair and with no end.

> You can shed tears that she is gone,
> or you can smile because she has lived.
> You can close your eyes and pray that she'll come back,
> or you can open your eyes and see all she's left.
> Your heart can be empty because you can't see her,
> or you can be full of the love you shared.
> You can turn your back on tomorrow and live yesterday,
> or you can be happy for tomorrow because of yesterday.
> You can remember her only that she is gone,
> or you can cherish her memory and let it live on.
> You can cry and close your mind,
> be empty and turn your back.
> Or you can do what she'd want:
> smile, open your eyes, love and go on.

I know I have shared this poem several times before, indeed I read it out at Claire's funeral but the reason I have shared it is because it is so true. I'm living my life now full of the love I shared with Claire, being happy for tomorrow because of everything she gave to me, I cherish her memory in photographs and in wearing my wedding ring and I let it live on in the same, I'm doing what she would want, smiling, opening my eyes, loving and going on.

> *"I still love you Claire and always will"*
> *xxx*

Tagged

- Wishing

87. Month 12 Week 52 Day 365 The End

It's been a year to the day that Claire left this world, a year to the day that my life changed irrevocably. It's been quite a journey this past year – many, many tears, much thought, much learning and a huge amount of reflection.

When I first started this blog I had no idea where it was going, all I knew was that I would use it daily to help me on my journey, that was what I did – but it's ended up being far more than that.

This website has connected people from around the world, each person that has contacted me has been put in touch with friends that are going through the same things. This has resulted in meeting some amazing people that have travelled from around the UK and the world to visit me and others – thanks especially to Grettel who travelled from New Mexico!

We've even had two people that lost partners become a loving couple as a result of meeting via this blog... yes, this blog has helped those in mourning and helped find love for those that have lost partners – I never expected any of that!

From a personal point of view this site has helped me over the loss of my lovely wife Claire, it has helped me come to terms with what it means to lose a loving partner... but I now know that I've turned a corner.

What I need to do now is to reclaim my life for my own. To work on ME, to begin to live life again – not as part of a couple with Claire, but as me... Mark, a unique and happy individual – and all of that is a very private and personal journey that will only be shared with people very close to me in my life. It's a natural stage to go through, and one that I must do without sharing publicly.

When I first registered this domain name I was aware that a time would come when it no longer felt appropriate. When I started I truly was lost without Claire, but now I feel different. I'm on a journey to finding the new me and so the word 'lost' doesn't fit with my journey any more and so this will be the last post I write.

It will be the last post, not because my journey is over, but because it is just beginning. It is beginning in a new vein, a new light and a new path. I'm no longer lost, I'm on a journey to being found and so it feels right to say goodbye to this part of that journey. I refuse to live life in the past, I will respect it and cherish those amazing happy memories and use those times to build a new life for myself.

I'd like to say thank you so much for your interaction with this blog over the past year – here are some stats that might amaze you – to date we've had:

- 36,880 visit to the site
- Visitors from 142 countries
- 6232 website shares
- 402 likes on Facebook
- 309 people comment on a post
- 24 people join a Facebook support group for the recently bereaved
- 2 people fall in love and begin to rebuild their lives together via the support group

And so, now it is my time to finish off this last post.

I will continue to grow.

I will continue to develop.

I will continue to live my life to the fullest possible with the love and support of those people closest to me, and if you are one of those people – thank you, I love you from the bottom of my heart!

Tagged

- The End

88. 2 years - 2 years

The last time I wrote a blog post was exactly one year ago. It's now two years since Claire passed away and I'm still getting so many people contact me as a result of this blog. So why am I writing another blog post two years to the day that Claire died?

When I first created this blog I didn't know why I did it. It just seemed like a natural thing to do, a natural thing to write and tell the world how I was doing. My head is clearer now, that mist of uncertainty has lifted and I'm clear about the purpose of this blog post.

Why write this?

2 reasons:

1. I want people to know that I'm okay.
2. I want people in my situation to know that their future can be bright.

It's only been two years but I honestly feel at peace. That's not to say I don't feel sad, that's not to say I don't miss Claire but it is to say that I feel at peace with the situation.

Feeling at peace is about accepting NOW as it truly is. But what is NOW?

I'm not talking about the big life picture, I'm not talking about feeling lonely (I don't by the way), I'm not talking about facing life without a wife, I'm not talking about money worries or any other worries... What I mean by NOW is this exquisite moment. This instantaneous and fleeting moment is all that we have in life. Every moment is unique and in isolation every moment has no worries at all.

If we think this moment does have worries it's because there is resistance. We are resisting one of two things:

Our memories from the past. These memories are flawed, they aren't the actual past they are just the way our brains have encoded sights, sounds & feelings. Those memories have bits missing and bits added and it's impossible for us to know which is which.

Our expectations of the future. Our expectations are flawed, they are created in our own head, they are illusions of the way we think our life should be.

Both our past and our future are constructions in our own mind. They are not reality, they either haven't happened yet or they are flawed re-creations of what has been. We worry when there is resistance and comparison between the past or the future and the NOW.

It's all created in our head. All of those worries don't exist in this unique moment. The instant we let go of comparing NOW, our worries disappear.

That's not to say that the life situation changes or gets resolved, but it is to say that the way we perceive that life situation changes dramatically. It becomes accepted as the way it is and the negative emotions surrounding that situation change, we can still take action to change the life situation but no longer feel the worry. It's like being stuck in the mud, if we panic and stress then the situation gets worse. The moment we calm down and accept that we are stuck in the mud, in other words we accept the NOW, we can begin to make a plan to change things in a calm and relaxed manner.

I came across this Buddhist poem recently and it's changed my life, it's called the "Four Reminders". The first verse is what got me...

> This human birth is precious,
> An opportunity to awaken.
> But this body is impermanent;
> Ready or not, one day I shall die.
> So this life I must know

As the tiny splash of a raindrop.
A thing of beauty that disappears
Even as it comes into being.
    The karma I create,
Shapes the course of my life.
But however I act
Life always has difficulties;
No-one can control it all.
Only acceptance of the now
can free me and others
From suffering forever.
    Therefore I recall
My heart's longing for freedom,
And resolve to make use
Of every day and night To realise it.

This human birth that we have all experienced genuinely is an opportunity to awaken. We can choose to use the opportunity to live in a world of negativity but I'm choosing not to. I'm choosing to accept that death is part of life. It's not natural to lose a partner so young, but our bodies are impermanent, ready or not one day we shall die.

So as I live my life as a tiny splash of a raindrop, knowing that as a thing of beauty it will disappear one day, I'm choosing to accept the now and free myself from suffering forever. I'm experiencing so many things in glorious technicolour, living each day moment by moment, noticing that this tiny splash of a raindrop is impermanent and will pass.

If you're friends with me on Facebook you'll probably notice my passion for food. Eating locally sourced and organic food has become a real passion. Every mouthful represents a single raindrop. Every mouthful is impermanent and it's a thing of beauty, I'm going to enjoy every one!

Okay, when I make a cup of coffee it takes me a while to get the water to 90°, then measure to get 15g of coffee to 250ml water, then wait for 2 1/2 min, then allow the temperature to drop to the perfect 42°... But I want to experience everything at its best, why settle for crap?

This birth is an opportunity to awaken, awaken to food, to life, to music, to experiences, to friendships, to rest, to holidays, to DANCING!...

If you're reading this, I implore you to make use of every day and night to realise your hearts longing for freedom, just as I am reminding myself to do right now as I remember my beautiful wife.

So, may the peace of God, which surpasses all understanding guard your hearts and minds forever. Xxx

Tagged

- Now
- Peace

89. What happens now?

Now you have come to the end of my ramblings you've come to the end of the journey in this book, and yet, as you have read and discovered the journey of grief has no destination... There is only the journey itself.

I challenge you to live each new day for the glory and beauty of that day, being thankful for yesterday and grateful for all that went before. This precious moment, right now is all that we have in life... There is nothing more than the present instant... So enjoy it, knowing that the love you shared endures...

Thank you for reading and please do join me on Facebook @lostwithoutherUK and Twitter @1lostwithouther [unique to this chapter in my life] or @markoborn [me being me]

Mark.

90. Index

About Mark

Mark runs currently a digital marketing agency and life coaching company. He has an MBA from the Open University and is a Master Practitioner of Neuro Linguistic Programming (NLP), Master NLP Coach, Master Practitioner of Time Line Therapy and Master Practitioner of Hypnosis.

He lives in West Dorset and enjoys dancing, wine & flying around the countryside on his motorbike.

He is a highly acclaimed public speaker with an engaging and fun style.

Please send media requests via www.lost-without-her.com

Lightning Source UK Ltd.
Milton Keynes UK
UKHW021202060720
366103UK00009B/243